Persuade

Using the seven drivers of motivation to master influence and persuasion

Philip Hesketh

CAPSTONE
A Wiley Brand

This edition first published 2016
© 2016 Philip Hesketh

Registered office
John Wiley and Sons Ltd, The Atrium, Southern Gate, Chichester, West Sussex, PO19 8SQ, United Kingdom

For details of our global editorial offices, for customer services and for information about how to apply for permission to reuse the copyright material in this book please see our website at www.wiley.com.

Wiley publishes in a variety of print and electronic formats and by print-on-demand. Some material included with standard print versions of this book may not be included in e-books or in print-on-demand. If this book refers to media such as a CD or DVD that is not included in the version you purchased, you may download this material at http://booksupport.wiley.com. For more information about Wiley products, visit www.wiley.com.

Library of Congress Cataloging-in-Publication Data

Hesketh, Philip.
    Persuade : using the seven drivers of motivation to master influence and persuasion / Philip Hesketh.
      pages cm
    Includes index.
    ISBN 978-0-85708-636-5 (paperback)
    1. Persuasion (Psychology)   2. Influence (Psychology)   3. Interpersonal communication.   I. Title.
    HM1196.H47 2015
    303.3′42–dc23   2015028023

A catalogue record for this book is available from the British Library.

ISBN 978-0-857-08636-5 (pbk)
ISBN 978-0-857-08637-2 (ebk)   ISBN 978-0-857-08638-9 (ebk)

Cover Design: Kathy Davis/Wiley
Hand drawn type: © Kathy Davis/Wiley

Set in 11.5/14.5pt Sabon by Aptara Inc., New Delhi, India
Printed in Great Britain by TJ International Ltd, Padstow, Cornwall, UK

Contents

Contents

Introduction: Our seven psychological 'drivers'

It's no secret that being part of a social group provides an all-important sense of belonging. For years, American Express has spent millions telling us that 'membership' has its privileges. But there is more to it. People believe a sense of belonging to a social group also gives their life more meaning.

But what's with this in-built desire to join social groups? In the animal kingdom the reason is easy to understand since it's mostly about survival. That's why wolves hunt in packs, birds fly together for safety and ants achieve more by working in unison.

Like Ant and Dec, for instance.

However, for humans, belonging to a group helps us form a view of our social identity which, in turn, contributes to our sense of who we are.

Back in the 70s, a famous study by Henry Tajfel demonstrated how complete strangers stuck together even when they had only the smallest thing in common. In his experiment, a group of boys were gathered together and then told they were to be split into two teams. Despite not knowing each other at all, most favoured being in a team with those immediately around them rather than those furthest away. Better the devil you know, I guess.

Tajfel was also able to demonstrate that merely putting people into groups – effectively categorizing them – is sufficient for people to discriminate in favour of their own group and against members of the other group.

It's a bit like meeting your countrymen abroad when on holiday. Walking along the promenade of a UK resort you would happily pass by without saying a word. But in a foreign country you're likely to at least exchange pleasantries when you recognize that they're from these shores. Wearing Union Jack shorts helps in this respect.

What's more, a funny thing happens when we join a group. We start to behave just like everyone else and follow the group 'norm'.

Even when there's nobody in the group called Norm.

One of the most famous experiments showing how easily we conform to unwritten group rules was conducted by Solomon Asch of Rutgers University in New Jersey. He asked participants to sit amongst a group of strangers and judge the length of queues that were being formed in front of them. What he didn't tell them was that all the other people had been instructed to lie when asked which was the longest queue. Sure enough, 75% of participants denied all the evidence from their own senses and instead conformed to the group view.

A similar experiment run by psychology professor Philip Zimbardo of Stanford University wasn't quite so successful. His idea was to place young men in a simulated prison environment with some assuming the role of prisoners whilst others played the part of guards complete with riot gear. Despite being a psychologist, he clearly hadn't thought through the consequences of the experiment and the likely long-term effects on the mental health of the participants.

To summarize, he recruited clean-cut young men as volunteers, none of whom had any kind of criminal record and who all rated 'normal' on psychological tests; and he randomly assigned half of them to play the role of prisoners and the other half to play guards. His plan was that he would step back for two weeks and observe how these model citizens interacted with each other in their new roles.

What happened next has become the stuff of legend.

Social conditions in the mock prison deteriorated with stunning rapidity. On the first night the prisoners staged a revolt and the guards, feeling threatened by the insubordination of the prisoners, cracked down hard. They began devising creative ways to discipline the prisoners, using methods such as random strip-searches, curtailed bathroom privileges, verbal abuse, sleep deprivation and the withholding of food.

Not surprisingly, many of the prisoners began to crack. It was clear that for everyone involved the new roles had quickly become more than just a game. Even Zimbardo himself felt seduced by the corrosive psychology of the situation. He began entertaining paranoid fears that his prisoners were planning a break-out, and he tried to contact the real police for help. Luckily, at this point Zimbardo realized things had gone too far.

After less than a week the experiment had to be scrapped when some of the 'prisoners' were becoming too submissive and some of the guards a little too zealous when meting out discipline. The prisoners were relieved; but tellingly, the guards were upset. They had been quite enjoying their new-found power and had no desire to give it up. Needless to say, the emotional fallout from the experiment outweighed any positive conclusions. In fact, I think some 'prisoners' are still on the roof protesting.

Only joking.

So if you want to join a group and become its leader, the first thing to do is conform. Then, when you feel trust has been gained, it's safe to start to show the way. And if you decide to start a group outside of work, don't forget to invite me. Because just like everyone else, I hate to be left out.

Today, people connect on LinkedIn and socialize on Twitter and Facebook partly to satisfy this need to be part of a group. The popularity of social media websites serves to underline this basic need in us all. Not just to share embarrassing pictures with the rest of the world, but rather to 'belong'. Outside of cyberspace, fans flock to football grounds to support their team in a show of unity. Even Brian, from Monty Python's 'Life of Brian', had his devoted followers whose overwhelming need to belong saw them follow him everywhere. Even though it turned out he wasn't the Messiah after all, just a very naughty boy.

There are seven psychological 'drivers' for us all. They are what make us 'tick'. Throughout the book we will explore these drivers and how, by understanding them, we can improve our relationships with the people around us, communicate better and get our own way more often. I have asked people all around the world 'What is most important thing in your life?' The answer is almost always 'My family'. And that is why the first three – and most important drivers – are to be loved, to be important and to have a sense of belonging.

But these are what drive all successful relationships – whether at work or with your friends. The word 'love' can mean so many things but often what it means in this context is that we want to feel that someone truly cares about us. It's why *you* need to show you are truly interested in the other person. And the word 'important' does not mean that you want to be the top dog. Rather, it means that people want to feel like what they are doing *matters*. That their contribution is valued.

In Greek mythology the greedy and deceptive Sisyphus was condemned to an eternity of hard labour. His task was to roll a great boulder to the top of a hill, but every time Sisyphus – after the greatest of exertion – reached the summit, the boulder rolled back down again and he had to repeat the task. It was the futility of it that took its toll. The exact opposite of the job having importance and mattering to someone was what really made Sisyphus suffer for his many crimes.

And Zimbardo's experiment in a simulated prison environment shows how quickly both the 'prisoners' and the 'guards' became part of a group. They started to behave as they did because their uniform told them they were part of a group. And they behaved like they thought other members of the group would behave.

We'll look more at these seven psychological 'drivers' throughout the book and show how, by understanding what makes us 'tick', we can not only be more persuasive and influential, but happier too.

So here are the top three drivers:

- We all want to be loved.
- We all want to feel important.
- We all have a deep-seated need to 'belong'.

Nat Lambert of Brigham Young University in Utah explored the implications of 'belonging' in an experiment where he asked participants to close their eyes and think of two groups to which they really belonged. Then they were asked about how much meaning they felt life had. The results were compared with those of two other groups where the participants were asked to think about something else. In one, they were asked to think about the value of other people, and in the other, the help that others had provided them.

The results showed that the participants who had been thinking about the groups they belonged to felt the highest levels of meaning in life. Proof that belonging to a group provides meaning over and above the value of others or the help they can provide.

But why is this? Well, it's more than just bonding. It seems that people who really feel like they fit in with others report the highest levels of 'meaningfulness' in their lives. I guess this is why the followers of some religious sects often seem like they have been brainwashed. A deep-seated and unshakeable belief in something often manifests itself in the strangest behaviour.

Think Tom Cruise jumping up and down on a chat show sofa.

Now stop.

Here's the really interesting bit:

People who feel that life is meaningful are more likely to be in good physical and psychological health. And – you guessed it – people who feel that life is not so meaningful are more likely to suffer depression and illness.

So it seems that there's a lot to be said for adopting a positive mental attitude, finding a real meaning in it all and socializing more.

And if you believe that, then you are much more likely to find true meaning in life because the need to *believe* is the fourth of the seven psychological drivers.

Indeed, success is most often achieved by those who just don't believe in failure.

Those words of wisdom came from none other than the stylishly elegant and fabulously chic Coco.

Not Coco the clown, of course, but the French fashion designer, Miss Coco Chanel. Her affirmation that anything is possible if you believe in it is a view shared by many a successful business entrepreneur.

But just how powerful is the act of believing and what part does it really play in determining success or failure? The answer may lie in a study by Irving Kirsch of Harvard Medical School, who conducted a series of trials featuring placebos. As I'm sure you know placebos are nothing more than sugar pills with no active ingredient that researchers use to test the efficacy of real drugs.

How and why placebos work is still something of a mystery. Some patients taking them report an improvement in their condition, some even claim to be suffering from the drug's side effects.

In a study of Parkinson's sufferers, it was discovered that placebo patients who reported an improvement had changes in their brain identical to those caused by the actual medication, Levodopa.

So why did these sufferers get better? Quite simply it was a case of mind over matter. They believed that what they were taking would help and so it did. Sportsmen and women use the same psychology to help them run faster, jump further and last longer. Some football teams believe they will score a goal in the last few minutes of a game and they often do. Aided by their opponent's belief in the very same outcome.

In his study, Kirsch reviewed the results from 35 clinical trials of modern antidepressant medication, such as Prozac, and concluded that placebos duplicated more than 80% of the improvement observed in the drug groups. In other words, 80% of people's improvement after taking a sugar pill they thought was Prozac was exactly the same as if they had actually taken Prozac. He also concluded that the effect of placebo on pain is about 50% of the response to pain medication.

So how does this phenomenon translate into the business world? Well, it seems to me that the vital ingredient is the expectation of benefit. In my work as a motivational speaker, I talk about these seven psychological drivers that we all possess – and, as I say, the fourth one is the need to believe. We all *want* to believe, we all *need* to believe. And it seems that if you believe enough, you'll go a long way to achieving your goals.

So here are the next four of the seven psychological drivers:

- The need to believe.
- The need for some certainty and some uncertainty in our lives.
- The need for 'a place'.
- The need for growth and improvement.

This need we have for some certainty and some uncertainty in our lives is all about having things to look forward to. If we know exactly how our life will be mapped out it takes away the fun and interest. But if we dread the future we have too much uncertainty in our life and are equally unhappy.

The first chapter in the book explores the psychology of having something to look forward to – and the role 'curiosity' plays in our lives – and the rest of the chapters in this book are crammed full of well-researched tips and techniques that help you improve your ability to relate to people, influence them and have a more successful and happier life. And that, in turn, makes you make feel more loved, more important and more acceptable to any group you want to be part of.

We'll cover the most successful persuasion technique there is, how to give better first impressions, how to make better decisions, avoid procrastination and increase the odds of people doing what you want them to do.

In other words it gives you 'more' – and that is why you are reading the book – for growth and improvement.

If you are typical, you sit in the same seat each night at home. You will probably have a favourite seat at your dining table. You might have a preferred seat on the bus, an area of the local bar where you and your friends meet. It's all down to this driver we have for 'a place'. A place we feel comfortable and we can call our own. It brings order and stability to our lives – it makes us feel comfortable – that is where we belong.

But for now, remember that the more you have a sense of 'belonging', the more meaning you will make of life.

All of the chapters refer not only to the 'drivers' but also to psychological experiments that give us real insights into why we do what we do and how you can get colleagues, clients and friends to behave more as you would wish them to.

And the final chapter summarizes the 'drivers' again; and how to live a happier and more successful life through a better understanding of our own behaviour.

1

Curiosity and the importance of having something to look forward to

There's an old saying that goes 'act in haste, repent at leisure'. Basically, it's a good idea to think things through before making a decision. Unfortunately, in today's high-speed, continuous, partial attention world, that's difficult. Salespeople implore you to take advantage of their soon-to-end discounts by signing today. What's more, you can often 'buy now, and pay later'. Sometimes, the repayments don't even start for another 12 months. However, the good news is you can do all your repenting from a comfortable new sofa.

Everything today is geared up to encouraging us to make a snap decision rather than one that is carefully considered.

Today, your other half only has to mention the possibility of a weekend in Barcelona and it can be booked online within the hour. But this 'buy now, pay later' culture can not only lead to economic difficulties, it can also actually reduce the pleasure we get from our purchases. You see, often, it's the anticipation of an event or a purchase that really gets our juices flowing. It's a sort of foreplay that consumers of old used to enjoy whilst watching their savings grow. Canadian psychologist Elizabeth Dunn calls it 'free pleasure'.

Dunn's research suggests that we get enormous amounts of pleasure just from looking forward to good things in the future. Like our summer holidays, for example. We all love to shop for new outfits, plan what we're going to do and imagine a lovely, warm sun beating down on our skin. Parties, celebrations, get-togethers and weddings. When describing their view of these events people often use expressions like 'I'm really looking forward to that' or, more confusingly 'I can't wait for that' when, of course, they have absolutely no choice but to wait. But it all shows the pleasure in the anticipation.

Fred Bryant of Chicago's Loyola University went one step further when he declared that not only do we get more pleasure by delaying purchases, we also make better decisions. Like not booking on the *Costa Concordia* cruise ship, or buying our Euros six months in advance.

But what if you can't wait and want it right now? What if you believe in living for today and don't care about tomorrow? There's a part of us that thinks we'll enjoy something more if we get it right now. But that's the greedy part of our mind and it's always proved wrong. You might think that what we lose in anticipation, we'll gain in reminiscences, since we have longer to enjoy our purchases. But this usually isn't the case. On the contrary, once objects or experiences are 'obtained' our mind forgets about them. But while they're still in the future, we keep mulling them over and the anticipation builds.

You may have experienced this feeling when changing your car. Often, you spend months weighing up all the options before deciding on the make and model, the trim level and the extras. It's all very exciting and you can't wait to take delivery. On the day you pick it up from the showroom you love the smell of the leather and are keen to keep it in pristine condition.

But then a few weeks into driving it, the novelty wears off and it becomes just another thing in your life that's expensive to run and difficult to keep clean. It's also why so many sporting events are a bit of a let-down. You spend ages looking forward to a major tournament and then two wins, two draws and a penalty defeat later you're left wondering what all the fuss was about. Similarly, it didn't really matter that a British male player didn't win Wimbledon for 77 years. Every year, we'd get out the flags and cheer them on in the hope that they might. That's the pleasure.

Because we are *curious* about the future. We want that balance between certainty and uncertainty.

Curiosity is what sent explorers off to discover the world. We are naturally inquisitive. It drives us, but we all need a balance too. And there's something else about curiosity that you need to know.

Curiosity may have killed the cat, but according to a neuroscience study, it plays an important role in boosting learning capacity. How so? I knew you'd be curious enough to want to know more. Well, it doesn't take an expert to work out that people are more likely to absorb information about topics that interest them. Not only do your ears prick up when your curiosity is piqued, but your brain is also sent a message along the lines of 'sit up and take note because this is going to be good'.

That's why ordinary people with standard IQ levels can go on TV game shows and answer questions about the past ten years of *Strictly Come Dancing*. Correctly. They know everything from at what stage a certain celebrity went out in 2009, to who was wearing a duck outfit in 2011. You would have to be a Strictly anorak to know all that – but for the sake of this chapter, let's just call them 'curious' people.

You see, scientists have discovered that our ability to remember incidental material is actually *enhanced* when presented to us at the same time as our curiosity is aroused. In other words, we remember more when we're doing or watching something we find interesting. That's why creative advertising works better than boring advertising. Remember Rab C. Nesbitt in the photo booth ad and the brand of cigar he smoked? Happiness is a cigar called? Similarly, many people can still recall the brand of beer that refreshes the parts other beers cannot reach. Twenty years later. And who could ever forget the brand of battery that powers the bunny rabbits in the TV ad? In short, if it's entertaining or interesting, we often remember it whether we want to or not.

To test the theory, three chaps called Loewenstein, Prelec and Shatto conducted a study. In the study, LPS asked people five questions on general knowledge and offered them a choice of reward. The choice was either a bar of chocolate, or to know the correct answers afterwards. When this choice of reward was offered *before* being asked the questions, 80% chose the chocolate bar. However, when it was presented to them *after* being asked the questions, 80% chose to know the answers. Why? Their curiosity had been piqued and they wanted to know how well they had done. Incidentally, nobody got the correct answer about the duck outfit.

Just like we want to look forward to things and events, we look forward to finding out 'what happens next'.

So how does all this help us in business? Well, if you have to make a presentation on a less than exciting topic, it pays to pique the audience's curiosity with some interesting facts and figures, or entertaining anecdotes. For instance, when I speak at conferences, I sometimes take a guitar on stage with me and leave it on a stand. Never play it. It's just there. A curiosity prop. Then my wife pointed out that the fact I don't play it could be to do with the power of several hundred people willing me not to go near it. Surely not. A curious thought though.

So if you are speaking at a conference make sure you pique the audience's curiosity. Don't just tell them what you are going to tell them – make them curious about what you are going to say.

If you are in a meeting and things aren't quite going your way with a potential client, say this: 'Can I ask you three questions?'

It will make them curious about what questions you have to ask. It's not just one question, but it's not 17 either which sounds like a questionnaire. The three questions you ask are:

1. What is the most important thing to you about … *(enter your key subject matter here)* … ?
2. What are your expectations exactly? (The word 'exactly' is very important as it asks for greater definition and clarity.)
3. If we were to … *(talk around their answers to questions one and two here and fulfil their desires and needs)* … would there be anything else we would need to consider?

The first question appeals to this need to be loved and important. The 'If we were to … ?' with the right answers reduces uncertainty for the prospect and shows there can be good growth and improvement (for them), and the constant use of 'we' rather than 'I' helps the feeling of belonging – that you are in this together.

If there is nothing else to consider then you can ask 'Shall we go ahead?' If there are other things to consider you can go over that ground until you are able to ask 'Shall we go ahead?'

And here's your next tip to get people to do what you want them to do. Often people don't do as you ask simply because they are too uncertain of their future if they do it. So ask them this simple question: 'Is there anything you are uncertain about?'

Listen carefully and genuinely see it from their point of view. Don't dismiss it just because it's something you are not worried about. Ask them how strongly they feel about that uncertainty. Ask them if there is more. Then, and only then, begin to reassure them.

And here's your final little tip for life on this issue of curiosity: try to always have something to look forward to, no matter how small. The power of anticipation in boosting your wellbeing is incredible. And you will make better choices for the future than if you make a snap decision right now. Today, we're like a small child looking at an ice cream. When choosing for the future, we're like sensible grown-ups, selecting things we know are better for us. Economists call this 'hyperbolic discounting', psychologists call it 'the present bias' and I call it the 'chocolate cake now, diet next week' effect.

2

Why keeping an open mind will help you to understand others

R ead this personality assessment and see how well it describes you.

You have a need for other people to like and admire you and yet you tend to be critical of yourself. While you have some personality weaknesses you are generally able to compensate for them. You have considerable unused capacity that you have not turned to your advantage. Disciplined and self-controlled on the outside, you tend to be worrisome and insecure on the inside. At times you have serious doubts as to whether you have made the right decision or done the right thing. You prefer a certain amount of change and variety and become dissatisfied when hemmed in by restrictions and limitations. You also pride yourself as an independent thinker and do not accept others' statements without satisfactory proof. But you have found it unwise to be too frank in revealing yourself to others. At times you are extroverted, affable, and sociable, while at other times you are introverted, wary, and reserved. Some of your aspirations tend to be rather unrealistic.

The assessment shown above was created by American psychologist, Bertram Forer, following his experiment on a group of students to assess their individual personalities. Of course, like most of the psychological studies you'll read about in this book, his experiment involved something of a deception. You see, he wasn't interested in assessing their unique personalities at all but rather how one, randomly-generated, piece of text fitted the students' own view of themselves.

The results were startling.

On average, students rated their 'individual assessment' as 85% accurate. Even though it was prepared in advance and the same result was given to every student.

This fake assessment was created simply by combining random snippets of horoscope readings. It demonstrates how easily people can be led to believe something even when it isn't true. This is relevant when studying the work of practitioners who use personality assessment as part of their trade.

The technique was even named after Bertram. Although it was later amended from the 'Cheating Lying Bastard Effect' to the more PC 'Forer Effect'.

Today, the term describes a person's tendency to interpret general statements as being accurate for them personally. This is particularly true when presented with a random personality assessment and being told it has been written especially for them. They simply look for anything that could be true and this influences them in rating the entire assessment as highly accurate. It's also the reason why a fortune teller need only get one small fact correct. Believers will latch onto this as proof that other facts yet to occur must also be genuine.

For instance, I can tell that as a small child you once grazed your knee in the school playground and had it lovingly bathed by a nurse Gladys Emmanuel type character. Okay, so maybe that last bit is my personal fantasy, but I bet the grazed knee bit is true. How do I know? Because it happened to us all.

If we analyse the structure of Forer's summary you'll see how the seven 'drivers' are covered. 'You have a need for other people to like and admire you' (Loved and important). 'You prefer a certain amount of change and variety and become dissatisfied when hemmed in by restrictions and limitations' (Balance of certainty and uncertainty). 'Some of your aspirations tend to be rather unrealistic' (Growth); and inbuilt in the whole thing is the desire and belief that someone understands you. And the reason 'you have found it unwise to be too frank in revealing yourself to others' is that you learned that the best way to belong to a group is to not reveal something that may cause rejection.

An experiment in 1979 by French statistician Michel Gauquelin proved the gullibility of people when interpreting horoscopes. He asked 150 participants to rate a horoscope reading for its accuracy in describing their character: 94% rated it as on the money. But, of course, the readings were again fake. In fact, all 50 participants had been given the horoscope of a serial killer named Marcel Petiot. It's fair to say that some of them were spitting blood when they found out. Another bizarre coincidence with Marcel.

The experiment didn't take place on April Fools' Day, but it might just as well have done.

On any given day it could be true that you do indeed encounter a tall, dark, handsome stranger. But he's just as likely to issue you with a parking ticket as sweep you off your feet. Which for most of us blokes is probably a bit of a relief.

The Forer effect is found in many areas related to the paranormal. For example, psychic readings, biorhythms and Tarot card sessions. You name it, it's working its magic in one way or another.

So this book dispels a few myths and relies only on proven evidence on what makes us more persuasive, happier, more successful and 'motivated'.

Fact is, the one thing that everybody wants is something you can give them quite easily.

To be treated as an individual.

There's a saying that you should never judge a book by its cover. Naturally, this isn't something that book cover designers embrace too readily. However, for the rest of us, it's a reminder that you should never form an opinion about something or someone based on appearances.

Think Susan Boyle.

Okay, you can stop now.

Instead, picture the beautiful young American student, Amanda Knox. In an eight-year period from 2007 to 2105 she was accused – then later found innocent – and then later found guilty again – and ultimately cleared of all charges – of the murder of Meredith Kercher, she was painted by the world's media as something of a femme fatale despite none of them ever actually interviewing her. All the initial assumptions about her were founded less on fact and more on the way that she looked and behaved.

I don't know whether she's guilty or innocent. What I do know is that if you read her book, *Waiting to be Heard* you will only draw one conclusion.

Her calm, care-free appearances in court were viewed by some as an act of callous contempt. Her sexy and provocative Facebook photos were interpreted by others as a sign of loose morals. As for the cartwheel in the police station – well let's just put that down to youthful exuberance and a touch of nerves. Put it all together and it's no wonder that we gorged on a series of lurid stories based on nothing more than hearsay, conjecture and wild fantasy.

So why is it that many of us believe we can tell a person's character just by looking at them, but at the same time are sure we can hide our own true character from others? Researchers at Groningen University in Holland coined the phrase 'illusory superiority' to describe this belief. In studies, they found that job interviewers tended to overestimate how much they thought they could learn of someone's character in a short meeting. Yet these same interviewers were certain that others could only get the merest glimpse of their character from such a brief encounter.

According to Nico Van Yperen and Bram Buunk, 'illusory superiority' leads people to believe: 'I am infinitely subtle, complex and never quite what I seem; you are predictable and straightforward, and I can read you like an open book.' (A word of warning: never say this to your partner if you want to watch the TV in peace.) Of course, this is further complicated when all we know of a person is what we've read in a magazine or seen on TV.

For one thing they're always a lot shorter in real life.

So for the world to make snap judgements about what kind of person Amanda Knox is, or what thoughts were going through her mind when she was pictured in court, is plainly foolish. Even four years later when she was photographed smiling whilst boarding a plane home, some interpreted this as the cat that got the cream. And not someone who was relieved that the nightmare was finally over.

So is there a business lesson to be learned here? Well, it seems that an inclination to oversimplify the minds and motivations of others lies at the root of most forms of inter-group conflict at work. People tend to think that those on 'their' side are reasonable, reflective and thoughtful, while those on the other side are not just wrong, but simplistic and dim.

Production don't believe the sales team understand them. The sales guys think the accountants are just trying to stop them doing their important job.

Deep down, of course, we know that others are as complex and difficult to read as ourselves. However, trying to figure out what others might be thinking is hard work. It requires intellectual application, empathy and imagination. So most of the time we don't bother and are happy to accept the stereotypes and prejudices presented to us by the media or our gut instinct.

In my view Amanda Knox revealed what kind of person she *really* is in her book. But perhaps the image of her smiling as she boarded the plane home will live longer in the memory of those who don't bother to read it. As for you, there's a very simple way that you can improve your ability to really understand people. Assume nothing. Keep an open mind. And ask more questions.

It's the person asking the questions who controls the conversation and the very quality of the conversation is dictated by the quality of the questions being asked. I have 50 what I call 'Killer Questions'. You'll find those at the back of the book. The majority of them begin with what, why, if, how and would. They're 'open' questions that allow people to talk about what is important to them. They allow people to talk about their beliefs. And all the time you are listening you are making them feel loved.

Chapter 2 is entitled 'Why keeping an open mind will help you to understand others'. As we have mentioned, what people really want is to be treated as an individual. Do you really know what matters most to the people who matter most to you?

Bertram Forer's personality assessment is not just a measure of how we can all be led to believe something even when it isn't true, it's a reflection of how we DO all have a need for other people to like and admire us. We DO tend to be critical of ourselves. We DO try and compensate for our personality weaknesses. We DO feel insecure and have serious doubts as to whether we have made the right decision or done the right thing. We DO think that there are times when we come over as introverted, wary and reserved.

So here is the top tip for improving and deepening your relationships with the people who matter most to you – both at home and at work. Appreciate their deepest thoughts are worries and concerns. Treat them like the individual they are and ask them questions that begin with what, why, if, how and would. 'Open' questions allow them to talk about what is important to them. And truly listen to their answers. And listen with the intention of understanding, not the intention of simply replying and providing an answer.

Fact is, most people think you are a great conversationalist when they are doing the talking.

3

Using the 'Bubble Reputation' to improve how others see you

Turning an acquaintance into a business associate is hard. Making them a friend is even harder. There are endless reasons why people fail to connect. And just like a marriage can break down, so too can the relationship between a client and a supplier. But how do you prevent it from happening?

Well you could start by sending more flowers and remembering birthdays. But in business? Psychologists tell us that we tend to like those people who disclose intimate secrets more than those who don't. It's a trust thing. After all, if someone's open enough about their penchant for cross-dressing, surely they wouldn't lie about their business plans? However, when someone you've only just met starts pouring out their heart to you, it's a different story. Rather than lend a sympathetic ear, you're more likely to want to change seats on the train or join another supermarket checkout queue. I mean, you only went out for a pint of milk, right?

However, it's also true that people disclose *more* to those they like. So if that rather odd-looking individual on the train happens to be a major buyer in your industry it's probably best to smile politely and hear him out. Similarly, people tend to prefer those to whom they have made personal disclosures. So again, stick with it.

The trick seems to be not to disclose too much, too soon, or too often.

Take internet dating.

Research suggests that the way internet daters reveal information about themselves provides clues to developing good relationships. Apparently, self-disclosure in terms of earnest conversations about your deepest hopes and fears is to be avoided. So no initial chat about global warming, quantitative easing or social unrest. Stick to your favourite music, food and books and a relationship will be formed more quickly.

Communicating online also gives you more control over the way you present yourself. Webcams excepted, nobody can see the nonverbal communication that a face-to-face conversation reveals. Like your nervous twitch, constant scratching, or lazy eye. Plenty of time for that over a candle-lit dinner. Truth is, it's far easier to construct an online identity with crafted emails and retouched photos. A study by Gibbs, Ellison and Heino concluded that successful online daters tended to use large amounts of positive self-disclosure, along with openness about their intent. The very opposite of many people's actual practice in online dating.

The idea that self-disclosure is important in relationships is no big surprise. But while it may be easy to understand in principle, the complexity of the process means it's much harder to do in practice. Generally speaking, it seems best to be open about yourself and honest and clear about your intentions. So don't be afraid to give of yourself if you want to build a good relationship with someone. But remember that the art of self-disclosure is about giving information to others in the *right* way and at the *right* time.

But just how 'familiar' should you be?

Does familiarity breed liking or contempt?

Imagine a big house populated by self-serving egotistical idiots with very little in the way of common sense or moral fibre. No, I'm not referring to the House of Commons, although I can see your point.

I allude, of course, to the TV programme *Big Brother*. Like it or loathe it, the audience figures suggest that plenty of people find it compulsive viewing.

Personally I'd rather watch paint dry. In fact, I think I saw that episode in series eight.

Now imagine if you were put in a similar house for a week with people you didn't know. Not a group of outrageous show-offs but ordinary people from all walks of life. A real cross-section with nobody weirder than perhaps a man with an unhealthy interest in steam trains who insists on sleeping with the lights on. How do you think you would get on with your house mates?

(A bit like an office environment really, where people from all walks of life are thrown together and expected to get on.)

Psychologists have long since assumed that familiarity actually breeds liking rather than contempt. The theory goes that the more people are exposed to each other, the more they discover the things they have in common, and the more they like each other. When I say 'exposed' I don't mean in the full frontal *Big Brother* sense. I mean discovering that you share a mutual interest in, say, flower pressing.

But a recent study by Michael Norton of Harvard Business School turned this theory on its head. His work concluded that the more you get to know someone, the more you discover the dissimilarities between you and the less you like them.

Think courtship, marriage, divorce.

Or best friends, holiday, nightmare.

So what is it that backs up Norton's theory and why is he staring so intently at me and my wife? Well, according to his theory, when we meet someone for the first time we look for similarities, and we typically find them. It may be a mutual interest in a sport, foreign travel, the arts, or stodgy desserts. Okay, so maybe that last one isn't a basis for a long-lasting relationship but it works for some. Unfortunately, after a while – say 250 servings – the assumption that this person is not only like us, but also likes us, starts to fade. And when this awful truth dawns, we like them less and begin to resent them eating so much of our cake.

So who's right? Well, in the studies where people interacted face to face, the more they interacted, the more they liked each other. Whereas in Norton's studies based solely on people's views on other people's preferences, the degree of liking was less. And perhaps more crucially, whether familiarity leads to liking or contempt seems to depend on our motivation. So, is it in your interests to get to know work colleagues really well and generate liking or should you keep your distance?

Well, as is often the case with these conclusions, it all comes down to balance. If you hang around with people for long enough, you'll eventually generate some mutual respect and discover common interests, even if they're not your type.

So get close, but not too close.

Be self-effacing and make personal disclosures. But don't allow them to know everything about you. Give them the firm impression that you are part of a 'cabal' – the feeling that you belong to a group, even if it's just a group of two.

And how do other people's expectations of us directly affect our own behaviour when we are part of a group? Being part of a group is one of our drivers.

In *As You Like It* William Shakespeare wrote that all the world's a stage and all the men and women merely players. Not bad for someone who never left England.

Of course what he was really saying is that life is all about relationships. And nowhere is that more true than in your world right now.

I added that last bit.

However, the question is not whether it is nobler to suffer slings and arrows. That's an easy one; avoid them at all cost. The *real* question is do we act our part simply to achieve our objectives, or are we influenced by how we *think* other people view us? To what extent do you play up to what is expected of you? If you think your reputation is one of the Class Clown do you subconsciously and automatically start to behave in that way?

Certainly people behave differently when they are in a crowd. We think and act differently than when we are on our own. Most people, if they observe some disaster or danger on their own – someone being being stabbed, a pedestrian slammed by a hit-and-run driver – will call for help and even risk their own safety to intervene. But if they are in a group observing the same danger, they hold back. Often it's simply because each individual assumes that nothing needs to be done because someone else has already taken care of it. And the more observers there are, the less likely any one person is to call for help. Psychologists call this process 'diffusion of responsibility'.

But it wasn't how people are affected by being in a crowd that Dr Mark Snyder from the University of Minnesota wanted to look at it. It was simply his idea that other people's *expectations* about us directly affect how we behave. Acknowledging that one of the quickest ways people stereotype each other is by appearance, he set up a series of 'blind dates' whereby couples chatted to one another via headsets but didn't actually meet.

Like most of these interesting psychological experiments I'm sharing with you in this book, a certain amount of sleight of hand was involved.

Two fistfuls in this case.

You see, psychologists know that it's human nature to assume that people who are very attractive are also more sociable, humorous and intelligent.

So, men were given a photograph of the woman they were going to chat to. Except, of course, the photograph wasn't genuine. Half were given pictures of women rated as very attractive and half of women who were rated as less attractive.

To arrive at the 'opinions' of which women were very attractive and which women weren't, they had previously had a wide range of men rate the 'attractiveness' of the women on a scale of 1 to 10, and only those ranked at least an 8 or at best a 2 were used in the study.

So, would the women pick up on the vibe given off by the men and unconsciously fit into the stereotype they had been randomly assigned? That's to say, would the 'beautiful' women actually be more friendly and sociable, and would the 'less attractive women' be dull and uninteresting?

On analysing the audio tapes, independent observers concluded that the 'attractive' women did indeed exhibit more of the behaviours stereotypically associated with attractive people: they talked more animatedly and seemed to be enjoying the chat more. In short, they conformed to the stereotype the men projected on to them. It seems people really do *sense* how they are viewed by others and change their behaviour to match this expectation.

Shakespeare was right.

The world is a stage. Expect your fellow players to like you and think well of you and you will improve the way they see you. Shakespeare called it the 'Bubble Reputation' in the same play – *As You Like It*. In the seven ages of man Jacques talks of the adult soldier stage being jealous in honour, sudden and quick in quarrel and seeking the bubble reputation. A bubble, of course, is empty; so by 'seeking the bubble reputation' Shakespeare means that a man does things that make him look good even if they are pointless. And it's still true today.

Understanding that other people's expectations of us directly affects our own behaviour means we have to be very careful when meeting a potential client or, indeed, anyone who we want to impress. Particularly if *we think* they don't like us. Because that negative vibe will influence their behaviour in a negative way.

On the upside, it also means that we can exert influence over the behaviour of others simply by changing our expectations of them. So if we *think* that they are going to place a big order, then they are more likely to do just that.

When I ran a business, young account managers would ask me: 'How do I become a director?' And I would reply: 'Start behaving like one now.'

So here's the top tip from this chapter. Create your own bubble. Behave like you are going to be liked. Behave like you are worth it. Don't be arrogant, but assume and believe that people will do what you want them to do.

4

How fleeting attraction and perceived similarity can change 'no' to 'yes'

'Oh would some power the gift to give us, to see ourselves as others see us!'

Of all the famous lines that flowed from eighteenth-century Scottish poet Robert 'Rabbie' Burns' quill, perhaps the one above still has the most resonance. I for one haven't worn a kilt since catching sight of myself in the wing mirror of a Ford Zephyr in 1974. I just don't have the knees.

In addition to the over-riding drives to be loved, important and belong, according to Estonian psychologist, Juri Allik, we also all still crave the gift to see ourselves as others see us. What's more, his research into the subject has turned up some interesting results about how closely our own perception of ourselves matches that of our friends and loved ones.

Allik and his researchers conducted personality tests on people from Europe, the USA, Japan and India. Each participant was asked to fill out a 'personality questionnaire' about themselves whilst someone who knew them well did likewise. Five different personality traits were considered: extraversion, neuroticism, agreeableness, conscientiousness and willingness to try new experiences.

Even across the different cultures, the results were remarkably similar. People were generally perceived by those closest to them as being less neurotic than they themselves thought. This suggests we appear less anxious, depressed or self-conscious than we feel. Also, people were generally rated as more conscientious and having greater competence and self-discipline than they gave themselves credit for. On the subject of extroversion and agreeableness, people were in general agreement. But generally speaking, people were rated as less open to experience, new ideas and values, than they thought. This perceived lack of adventure even extended to our fantasies, which is a real eye-opener given that you can't be prosecuted.

Here's the paradox. We know that most people consider themselves to be above average when compared to others. But clearly we can't all be right. However, unlike most of our comparisons which are against strangers, Allik's study consisted of friends and family. Perhaps these results suggest our loved ones have a natural positive bias towards us which leads them to rate us higher than a stranger on socially desirable personality traits. Who knows? Well, if anyone should, they should.

The bottom line is that, on average, our friends and loved ones have much the same view of our personality as we do. Perhaps we are a little pessimistic on neuroticism and conscientiousness, maybe a little optimistic on our desire for new experiences. But heave a sigh of relief. They see the real you.

Just keep that fantasy under wraps.

And does how well somebody knows you affect your ability to influence them?

Well, it's much easier to persuade family or friends to do something than it is a complete stranger.

There's an unspoken commitment to helping people we know.

But perhaps more interestingly, in business there's even a propensity to help people we've only just met if we discover that we have something in common.

For example, we've all got talking to a stranger in a bar about, say, sport and discovered we favour the same team. Within minutes there's a bond. We 'belong' partly because we have the same belief. We're also, in that scenario, sharing a place. My wife and I had a lovely holiday in Fiji recently and have kept in touch with the four other couples despite the thousands of miles between us because we shared an experience (we were the only 10 people on an island resort). We 'created' a group and we shared 'our' place for a week. And because of that common bond we are more than willing to help each other.

I have two major banks as clients all because I met Paul Bruton when we studied at Harvard University back in 2011. Paul and I formed our own 'cabal'. We shared an experience and when his daughter was over in the UK doing an internship at a major bank she asked me to come and talk to a group at the bank. That led on to more work and ultimately to me speaking to another bank. I'm sure you have similar stories.

The question is: how much does someone have to like us before we can start to influence their behaviour? Well, the answer comes from a study by Jerry Burger at Santa Clara University. This one doesn't just use the usual sleight of hand but is also admirably sneaky too. In the experimental set-up, participants were told the study was about first impressions and were asked to choose 20 adjectives which best described them from a list of 50.

The idea, they were told, was that they would swap and compare their list of adjectives with that of another participant. However, unbeknown to them, the list that they were given from the so-called 'other' participant had been manipulated. By using what psychologists rather imaginatively call the 'mere similarity' effect, participants were given lists that either closely matched or varied greatly with their own.

Some had ticked only three adjectives the same as the 'other' person and so the perception was that they had very little in common. Some had selected 10 of the same adjectives and so were considered to be neutral.

But then there was a small group who believed that the other person had chosen 17 adjectives that they themselves had selected. On the face of it, they had a lot in common with the 'other' person thanks to the researchers manipulating the results. But would it make them more likely to do something for that other person? After all, we know from basic psychology that people like people who are like themselves.

The second part of the experiment provided the results.

The participants were then introduced to the person with whom they had swapped lists. Or so they were told. Naturally, this 'other' person was a member of the research team. After a brief chat, came the moment of truth. The researcher, in passing, asked the participant if they would do them a favour. They asked them if they would mind reading an eight-page essay and then provide a page of feedback? Naturally, not many people would be keen to do this rather onerous chore for someone they had only just met. Yet 77% of those who had selected 17 out of 20 adjectives the same, obliged. One even offered to clip the person's toe nails and perform a back wax.

Only kidding.

Of those whose results made them appear to be dissimilar to the other person, only 43% said yes to providing the feedback. Fewer still said they would be happy to trim body hair of any sort.

Just kidding again.

So, what have we learned? Well, it seems that fleeting attraction and perceived similarity can be remarkably powerful in changing 'no' into 'yes'. Whilst relatively small requests are processed in an automatic way using simple rules of thumb, when it comes to considering the same request from a stranger we make a snap judgement based on trivial information and how much we like them.

If we feel they are 'like us' we also think we 'belong' to a group of like-minded people with the same values and beliefs.

So the next time you need a favour from a perfect stranger, be sure to point out the similarities between you before you ask. I do it on trains all the time. It really does work.

And remember, people think you are less neurotic, anxious, depressed and self-conscious than you feel.

And finally in this chapter, how do people's opinions of you impact on your ability to influence them? Well, providing positive feedback as a means of encouraging people to try harder is nothing new. If people think you think well of them and you are encouraging they are more likely to carry on with that behaviour and like you more. Teachers, sports coaches and parents alike all use this technique to get the best out of youngsters. Many a football dad had spent a rain-soaked

Sunday morning shouting words of encouragement to his youngster who has just missed his third sitter in a row. 'Keep your chin up and your head down next time, son!' Even the Elephant Man would struggle to do that.

Now, a study by Gary Wells and Amy Bradfield at Iowa University reveals exactly how people's behaviour can be influenced when they are given positive feedback. In their experiment, participants were shown an 8-second clip of low-quality CCTV footage of a store being held up at gunpoint. The clip was from a genuine raid and had been slowed down so that the participants could get a good look at the robber. After watching the footage, the participants were told that the man had shot dead the security guard during his escape. This was not caught on camera but the incident was true and a man was subsequently caught and convicted of the crime.

The job of the participants – or so they thought – was to identify the killer from head shots of five suspects. Herein lies the deception. The participants think that the experiment is about their powers of observation, not how they might be influenced by positive feedback. Hence, each group was told that the real killer was in the line-up when, in fact, he had been removed. All the men shown were innocent of the crime.

Each of the participants identified the suspect they thought had been the gunman. Regardless of who they picked out, the real experiment then began when they were given 'false' feedback on their decision. As a control, one group was given no feedback at all. The second group was told that they had picked the wrong man, whilst the third group was 'congratulated' on choosing the correct suspect. Which, of course, they hadn't.

This is where the study gets interesting. Participants were then asked to describe how *easy* it was to identify the suspect and make out his facial features, and how *certain* they were of picking out the right man. The group given no feedback at all thought the identification process was hard, the footage not very clear, and the facial features not visible enough to make a positive identification. Not surprisingly, the group who had been told they had chosen the wrong man, echoed this first group's sentiments.

However, it was a different story for the group 'congratulated' on correctly identifying the killer. They thought that the identification process was easy, that the killer's features were clear, and that their judgement was accurate and trustworthy. Perhaps most chillingly, they were all so confident of their choice that they were willing to testify in a court of law. In effect, the positive, yet false, feedback had convinced them they were correct.

It's easy to see how miscarriages of justice can happen with simply a nod of approval, an encouraging smile, or some such positive body language from a prosecutor. Of course, in business, and at home, it means that if you want people to carry on doing good work, you simply need to keep on rewarding them with positive feedback. You need to make them feel loved, that what they are doing is important, that they are a valued member of the team, that they are contributing to growth and that they have a place in the grand scheme.

Start telling people what you like about them – particularly the ones that you love. Catch people doing something right and give them a word of encouragement and thanks. And when you meet someone new, mention the things you have in common. It's the similarities that draw us together and the differences that make us interesting. Fact is, perceived similarity can be remarkably powerful in changing 'no' into 'yes'.

5

The single most persuasive expression you can ever use

There's one persuasion technique that has been consistently shown to work in almost any situation. It's very practical, can be used by anyone and doesn't involve a carrot or a stick. In the US it's known as the 'But you are free' technique. In the UK we'd probably say, 'It's up to you' or 'You are free to choose'.

Why does it work so well? Because it tags onto the end of your request a phrase that reaffirms people's freedom to choose. You're not forcing them to do something, you're simply asking them politely and then reminding them that they've got a choice.

Their choice.

When my sons were young I would use this technique to stop them swinging from a dangerous tree, trying to jump over a fast-running stream, or just to discourage them from testing the temperature of a domestic appliance by holding it against their bare skin. 'I wouldn't do that if I were you. But it's up to you,' I would say. Okay, so maybe it didn't always work but, on the upside, I did get good value out of the Harrogate and District Hospital A&E service.

But generally speaking, it works a treat. Probably because none of us likes to be 'persuaded'. By adding 'It's up to you' you are indirectly affirming a person's freedom to choose. In effect, you're not threatening their right to say 'no'. Christopher Carpenter of Western Illinois University carried out research in this area involving some 22,000 people. What he discovered was that simply adding the phrase 'But you are free ...' *doubled* the chances of people saying 'yes' to a request. The only phrase that achieved a higher success rate was 'Or I'll kill all your family'.

Just kidding.

But that would probably work too.

So where's the proof? Well, people have been shown to donate more to good causes, agree more readily to take part in a survey, and give money to someone asking for a bus fare home, simply by adding that phrase. The exact words are not especially important. 'Totally your choice' works. As does 'But obviously, don't feel obliged'.

When most people would then actually feel more obliged.

The important thing is that the request is made face to face, otherwise the power of the technique diminishes. It sometimes works via email, but less so than when delivered in person. What this really underlines is that we don't like to be hemmed in and have our choices reduced. That only serves to make us even more closed-minded.

As with all effective methods of influence rather than persuasion, this whole technique is about 'helping' other people come to the decision you want through their own free will. They need to feel like it was *their* decision. And it means they are less likely to change their mind later. Respecting people's autonomy has the happy side-effect of also making them more open to influence rather than persuasion.

And there's another key way to get people around to your point of view:

Let them do the talking.

Persuading people around to your way of thinking is a difficult task, particularly if they've already made up their mind.

We talked in the introduction about the fourth 'driver' – the need to believe. And once we form a belief we only look for evidence to support the belief. And that, in turn, becomes even more fixed in the mind.

This stubborn intransigence manifests itself in all manner of life. From the child who won't eat up his greens to the bun fights in the House of Commons.

It's the reason heart-felt petitions are filed straight into the bin, and it's also why football fans believe that playing at home in the second leg of a two-legged game provides a better chance of winning the tie. But it's simply not true if you take a closer look at the stats. Which is exactly what a formidable sounding midfield trio of researchers from Munich University did. Herrs Eugster, Gertheiss and Kaiser studied the results of European ties between 1994 and 2010 and discovered that the chances of winning are exactly 50:50, whether you play at home first or second. Unless, of course, it goes to penalties when the stats show that the British teams are all but doomed.

Despite this fact, football fans continue to travel to the away leg of their two-legged European tie with the cheery thought that no matter what disaster befalls them, they can turn it around in the home tie. 'We've done it before, we can do it again.' Why such confidence? Well, because like most long-held beliefs, once an opinion is formed, we look for as much evidence as possible to support it. Even if the stats don't really add up.

You see, we resent having our attitudes adjusted by others, and so resist it at all costs. So it's best if people change their own minds. It's difficult to do it for them. People will listen to themselves and automatically generate arguments that have personal relevance. It's called self-persuasion and the theory was tested by two researchers from Yale University.

Despite sounding like a hairy pop duo from the early 70s, Janis and King managed to persuade students to take part in an experiment that didn't involve smoking anything first. Instead, all they had to do was give a talk on a subject to two of their fellow students to try to persuade them about something. Then they swapped things around so each student had a turn at giving the talk.

Janis and King discovered that the students were more convinced by the talk that they gave themselves than when they listened passively to the same argument put forward by their fellow students. This suggests that we really are persuaded more strongly when we make the argument ourselves, even if it isn't in line with our own viewpoint. That's probably why it's a good idea to rehearse speeches and presentations out loud – not just to hear how it sounds but to make the final performance all the more convincing.

Pablo Briñol of Madrid University added more weight to the theory when he studied attitudes to smoking. He found that people were more likely to be put off smoking when they delivered an anti-smoking message themselves than when they passively received it. Simply saying it out loud was more convincing.

So here's how to get someone to come around to your way of thinking. Simply ask them to put aside their own attitude and beliefs for a moment and try to see it from your point of view. Then ask them to argue the case as if they were – hypothetically – holding your beliefs.

Use expressions like 'Just out of curiosity, if you were to argue the case what would you say?' or 'Hypothetically, how would you put forward the case if you were me and were trying to convince others of the argument?'

Before you know it, by generating their own arguments on the subject, they will be more inclined to your way of thinking and to changing their mind.

And there's more.

'While we teach, we learn,' said the Roman philosopher Seneca. It's a fact that students enlisted to tutor others work harder to understand the material, recall it more accurately and apply it more effectively. In what has been dubbed the 'protégé effect,' student teachers who are learning to teach score higher on tests than pupils who are learning only for their own sake. And it's partly the greater commitment to learn the material and partly that they talk themselves around to a particular point of view.

How do you increase the odds of people doing what you want them to do?

The quote often attributed to Benjamin Disraeli is 'there are lies, damned lies and statistics'. By which he meant – if it was him that first said it – that you can manipulate just about any set of figures to make them sound far more impressive. Over the years, marketing people have exploited this technique many times to beef up a proposition.

For instance, there's a well-known brand of cat food that eight out of ten owners say their cat prefers. That sounds like 80% of cats prefer it. But, of course, it just means that 80% of the 100 or so cat owners who took part in the survey *think* their cats prefer it. In other words, less than 0.01% of all cat owners say that their cats prefer it. Not as impressive when the stats are presented this way, is it? Or am I just being catty?

Similarly, like me, you may well be sitting on the edge of your sofa every Saturday hoping and praying for your balls to drop. You're no doubt watching the lottery, whereas I'm just a late developer. Of course, by now, everyone knows that the odds of winning the jackpot are 14 million to 1. Yet we still think it's worth a punt.

Statistically, there's more chance of being eaten by a shark.

Even if you live in my home town of Harrogate in North Yorkshire.

One minute you're sipping tea in Betty's, the next minute all the crumpets have disappeared along with your lower limbs. It could happen. And it could be you.

In every betting game, the odds are against the player. That means that the 'house' (the casino, bingo hall, racetrack, lottery commission, etc.) is absolutely guaranteed, mathematically, to win over time. For every millionaire created from lottery winnings, there are many millions of others who have lost their money.

And the longer you gamble; the more likely you are to lose.

Many people who develop problems associated with their gambling have the false belief that they will be able to 'beat the system', while others may not understand that the odds are just against them and that over time they will lose money.

You are more likely to be killed by lightning (1 in 56,439) than win the lottery. You are more likely to be killed in a traffic accident driving 10 miles to purchase a ticket than win the jackpot.

Imagine you are standing blindfolded on a football field holding a pin. A friend has released an ant on the field. Your chance of hitting that ant with your pin is about 1 in 14 million, the same odds of winning the Lotto 6/49 jackpot.

So why do we buy lottery tickets so avidly when, for the organizers, it's little more than a licence to print money? The answer is because it cleverly exploits a simple weakness in the way the human mind works. Called the 'availability bias', it's the tendency that we have to judge probabilities on the basis of how easily examples come to mind. So it doesn't matter that the odds of winning the lottery are very long; the fact is we hear about yet another lucky jackpot winner every week. Hence, we assume that we're much more likely to win than we really are.

When I speak at conferences and ask delegates to guess the percentage of UK households consisting of a husband, a wife and two children – a boy and a girl – they always overestimate wildly. This is because they are so used to seeing the 'typical' nuclear family in TV dramas and in advertising they think it's more common than it really is. The actual figure is less than 4%.

When people in the USA were asked by Brian Paciotto to estimate the number of deaths per 200 million US citizens, 'drowning' figured higher than death by fireworks, tornados and asthma put together. Yet the actual figures were very similar indeed.

People felt they had read more about people drowning – could possibly imagine death by drowning more easily than the other three options – so assumed that it would be more common.

So how can you exploit the 'availability bias' to influence the behaviour of others? Well, you can start by reminding them how common it is to benefit from what you want them to do. Tell them that the decision they are about to make is a very popular one, that what they are about to purchase has been bought by several people very recently. Travel websites often tell us that there are only one or two seats or rooms available at this price – inferring many have bought. They also inform us of how many people are looking at the particular item at that time.

'Join the thousands whose eyesight has already been restored with laser eye surgery' might be your slogan if you're a laser eye surgeon. If you're a tree surgeon, this doesn't work at all.

It makes you think you are part of a group. A group of people who have made a good decision and it would be a good idea to be part of that group. It takes away the uncertainty and reassures you.

So to influence people's behaviour, rather than persuading them you need to let them think they have made the decision. That they were 'free to choose' – that they talked themselves into that way of thinking. And you do that by asking questions. As I've already mentioned, the majority of my 50 'Killer Questions' at the end of the book start with words that make them open questions that ask the other person to give you information.

So, to recap, don't criticize other people's beliefs but, rather, ask them how they arrived at their belief. Ask them – just out of curiosity – if they were to argue the case 'what would you say?' Let people know how common it is to benefit from what you want them to do; that the decision they are about to make is very popular with others.

Most importantly, let people think they have made the decision themselves.

6

How to worm your way into a group's affections and influence them

If you've ever been the new kid on the block, you'll know how difficult it is to have your views accepted by the 'established group'. For instance, imagine you've joined a new company and you're attending a think tank to discuss a problem which is new to them, but old hat to you.

Something you experienced and dealt with in your previous job. In theory, your views should be welcomed with open arms. But, in practice, it's more likely to be open mouths. Who does this upstart think he is? He's only been here five minutes ...

This group behaviour is what psychologist Matthew Hornsey from the University of Queensland calls 'unreasoning hostility'. It consists of having your views largely ignored or overlooked.

In my house it's called parenting.

Anyway, to test the theory, Matthew's researchers asked 200 health professionals for their opinions on criticism levelled at their hospital by an independent observer. However, whilst one half were led to believe that the critic was a newcomer who had worked there only three weeks, the other half were told that it was the views of someone who had worked at the hospital for 18 years. Naturally, the criticisms were identical, with the only difference being the apparent source.

As suspected, the views of the 'newcomer' were thought to carry less weight than those of the 'old-timer'. What's more, their criticism was also seen as *less* constructive whilst their suggestions were more readily dismissed by the health professionals.

It's one of the ways groups form their opinions, by 'polarizing' their views. A handful of people feel very strongly that the view of the newcomer is wrong and fellow members of the group – who didn't feel quite so strong initially – become more and more convinced of the 'team view'.

So, as a newcomer, how do you worm your way into a group's affections and begin to generate influence? The answer is to tread carefully and gain acceptance *first*. Once you become part of the group you can begin to make all manner of recommendations, however absurd. Newly appointed cabinet ministers are prime examples. For instance, you wouldn't ask the Minister for Transport for expert advice on a schools matter. You'd wait until the Cabinet reshuffle next week and ask him when he's Minister for Education.

Bottom line is you have to be part of the group. A fully paid-up member of the club. One of them. You 'belong' as much as they do. You see, consciously or otherwise, people want others to value *their* group as much as *they* do. They see their group as important. So distancing yourself from an old group or employer increases your perceived allegiance to the new one. And criticism from a committed group member is seen as much more valid. In effect, it sweetens the bitter pill of reality.

Of course, the temptation when joining a new group is to try to make a big splash and impress others with your critical perceptions and new ideas. But this research tells us that toeing the line in the first instance is often the best long-term strategy. Remember, groups are hostile to criticism from newcomers and are likely to resist, dismiss or ignore it. Until you can prove your loyalty.

So if you're a newcomer and want to gain influence and promote change in your new surroundings, make sure you get well established first. Because sometimes being right just isn't enough.

And if you should ever find yourself standing in the dock, cross your fingers that you are tried by one solitary judge rather than a panel of three. Because research into 1,500 trials in the US by Thomas Walker and Eleanor Main has shown that when judges sit alone they take an extreme course of action only 30% of the time.

But when sitting in a group of three this figure more than doubles to 65%.

So why is this? Well, again, it's the phenomenon known as 'group polarization'. And it's one that's not only present in courts of law but also in your workplace too. The only difference is that you don't occasionally send an old lady to jail for 20 years just for holding up the queue in the post office.

Conventional wisdom used to suggest that whenever any group of people arrives at a joint decision, that decision would broadly represent the average view of the individuals – thus averaging out the extremity of views. However, a whole body of psychological research has turned this theory on its head. Instead, it concludes that group discussions tend to *polarize* a person's view, making it more exaggerated and extreme.

For instance, few people know this, but the panel who tried Joan of Arc were originally planning to let her off with just a fine. It was only after a series of heated discussions that they concluded, 'on second thoughts, let's torch her'.

It's the same in other situations. After a group discussion, people who already support a war become more supportive; people with a tendency towards racism become more racist; and those with a slight preference for one job candidate over another will end up with an even greater preference for that candidate as more and more people 'polarize' towards the candidate.

Once that tendency or inclination becomes a fully fledged belief, people look for evidence to support the belief they've developed. And the more colleagues around them support the belief, the more entrenched it becomes.

So how can you use this knowledge to your advantage? Well, in group discussions we know that individuals who don't initially agree with the consensus of opinion will eventually agree with the majority. Sure, some may be swayed by a rational counter-argument, but most will eventually conform to the view of the group. Couple that with the desire to make the sort of impactful decision that a committee is expected to make and decisions are pushed further towards the extreme.

(Sarita Yardi of Georgia Institute of Technology, Atlanta and Danah Boyd of Microsoft analysed 30,000 tweets on Twitter regarding the shooting of George Tiller, a late-term abortion doctor. Again, they found that like-minded individuals *strengthen* group identity, whereas replies between different-minded individuals reinforce a split in affiliation. People will group together based on opinions and polarize in one direction even when they haven't met.)

So here's what to do if you want to influence a group of people.

Lobby beforehand.

Give them the rational argument prior to the meeting. Politicians have lobbied for centuries because they know that you need as many people as possible leaning to your point of view from the outset.

But before we leave this chapter, let's examine the counter-argument of working hard to get well established and ingratiating yourself into the hearts and minds of a group or, indeed, an individual. The psychology of 'Playing hard to get' ...

Life is full of 'if onlys'.

Take the course of history. It's littered with hundreds of moments that could have led us down a completely different path – if only ...

For example, if only Brutus had been a bit more loyal to Caesar, what might the world map look like today?

If only Thomas Farriner had been more vigilant with his baking, London may not have burned. Just a keener sense of smell might have sufficed. And if only Anne Boleyn hadn't played hard to get with Henry VIII who knows what the British monarchy might look like today.

All too often, the problem is that we're tempted by the taste of the forbidden fruit rather than what's on a plate in front of us. Think Anthony and

Cleopatra, Scarlett O' Hara and Rhett Butler, Simon and Garfunkel. On second thoughts, strike that last one out, I got carried away.

But is playing hard to get a fact or simply an urban myth coupled with an old wife's tale? And if you are in the business of wooing, should you play hard to get? Well, psychologist Elaine Walster and her cohorts at the University of Wisconsin conducted an experiment to discover just that. She recruited five single men who were each looking for a female partner. It was a kind of 'Blind Date' but in a laboratory rather than in front of a live studio audience.

The men were each given a profile to study of five women all with very similar attributes. That is to say, they all had similar interests, levels of education and careers, and none stood out from the others for being particularly beautiful or plain.

Oh, and there was one other thing. None of them actually existed in real life. The photos were of other consenting researchers and the profiles were entirely made up. In short, they were wholly fictitious women.

I don't know about you but I'm attracted already. Think of the money you could save.

The men were each told that the computer had 'matched' them with these five women and that the women had also studied their profile and that of four other suitors. However, before being asked to choose a date, each guy was told the following about each of the women's reactions after studying all five of the men's profiles:

One woman had given high ratings to all five men, thus placing her in the category of 'easy to get'.

One woman had liked their profile in particular but none of the other four men, thus placing her in the category of 'selectively hard to get'.

One woman didn't like any of the men, thus placing her in the category of 'always hard to get'.

And, finally, two of the women declined to give any clues about which men they did or didn't like, thus placing them into the category of 'no information'.

Armed with this information, the men then made their choice. Perhaps not surprisingly, one woman was far and away the most popular; the one who was described as 'selectively hard to get'. That is to say, easy for them, but hard for everyone else. In fact, this woman polled more than double the votes of everyone else put together. I've got her phone number if you want it.

So why is this? Well, apparently, most men thought that the selectively hard to get woman would combine all the advantages of the easy to get woman with none of the drawbacks of the hard to get woman. They thought she would be popular, warm and easygoing, but not demanding and difficult. Much like my wife, who kindly contributed this one sentence to the chapter. But most of all, she represented someone who to others was hard to get, but for him, was actually quite easy.

So showing selective interest is proven to be the best strategy when wooing a partner or potential client.

Influencing groups of people is about understanding the nature of the cabal. It's about respecting their views and beliefs. Lobbying prior to the group meeting is as old as the hills but key to getting your own way. And playing slightly hard to get? Well, it makes the other person feel special.

It worked for Anne Boleyn.

At least before she lost her head.

So what are the key issues arising from this chapter? Well, if you are a newcomer to a group it's best to slowly work at being accepted and work your way into a group's affections before you begin to generate influence. Tread carefully and gain acceptance first. And if you are going into a meeting and you want to influence a group of people – lobby beforehand.

7

The 'chameleon effect' and how to use body language to your advantage

Whenever I speak at conferences, the delegates tend to fall into three categories. Those in a trance, those in a deep sleep, and those who are fully comatose.

Only kidding again. No, really, I am.

The truth is, there are those who sit up nice and straight, obviously eager to maximize their learning. Always bright and alert, I call them the sheep dogs. After those come the ones who are slightly sceptical about learning anything useful, but are nonetheless willing to give you the benefit of the doubt. Often they lean backwards in their chair, surveying the room in the manner of a guard dog, just waiting for the occasional tasty tit-bit to be tossed their way. And then there are the mongrels. The cross between a hound dog and a St Bernard. They slouch in a slovenly manner and give the impression of not being interested in anything. Their body language tells you they really don't want to be there.

I remember from my school days that it wasn't cool to be seen sitting up straight and paying attention. In fact, if you wore two matching socks you were considered posh. But apart from indicating your attitude to the situation and your willingness to take part, does sitting up straight and not slouching actually influence how much you learn? Does the way you sit at a sales meeting or a marketing conference actually make a difference to what you take away from the event?

Well, a study by Pablo Briñol of Madrid University examined how people's self-confidence and self-evaluation are affected by the pose they strike. He divided a class of students into two groups: half were told to slouch whilst the other half were asked to sit up straight. They were given some cover story about the experiment being concerned with curvature of the spine to throw them off the scent. These two groups were then split again, and half were asked to write down three positive personal traits about themselves, whilst the other half had to write down three negative personal traits.

So they finished up with four groups of people. The ones who slouched and wrote positive things about themselves; those who slouched and wrote about their negative traits; the ones who sat up straight and wrote positive things about themselves; and finally the ones who sat up straight but noted down three negative personal traits.

The results showed that people who had been sitting up straight were much more likely to *believe* the positive things they'd written about themselves, whereas those who were slouching were much less sure. In short, their posture actually affected whether they really believed the positive or negative things they wrote about themselves. Proof that what you decide to do with your body position actually feeds back to your brain and ultimately affects your thinking.

So when you're at a conference or sales meeting, you should sit up straight with your shoulders back, and don't slouch. Because you won't just be giving the right impression, you'll probably learn a lot more too.

And there's more.

Being in a position of power is something that most business people crave. But a strange thing happens the higher you go up the corporate ladder. There's often a rope waiting at the end of it. Of course, nobody means to commit business or political suicide; it's just that the single-mindedness that got them there can also work against them. Convinced of their own infallibility and importance they begin to make odd decisions. Ones that they don't question and don't welcome others doing so either. World history is littered with egotistical despots – not to mention the odd former chancellor – who got too full of themselves. I'm not talking Hitler there either.

According to Julia Fischer of Munich University, the secret of making better decisions is to relax. Her study revealed that when you adopt a more neutral pose, like maybe resting an elbow on the table, and keeping your hands visible and relaxed, you are more likely to take onboard another person's view and make a more informed decision. On the other hand, making any kind of obscene hand gesture is considered most unhelpful. Make that either hand.

Obviously a positive body language helps you give a better first impression too.

Walk tall, walk straight and look the world right in the eye. That's what Jonny Cash's mama told him when he was about knee high – and it's still pretty good advice today. But here's the twist. If you've got an interview, you need to adopt that stance right from the off. As you walk into the building. As you pace manfully – or womanfully – through reception. As you stride confidently into the room.

Because afterwards, when the interview actually begins, it counts for nothing. In a study by Amy Cuddy of Harvard Business School, it was proven that students who adopted expansive, high-power postures made the better impression and were more likely to be chosen for the job. Adopting power postures during the interview had no effect. You have to relax, remember. But if you still don't get the job it is permissible to crawl out of the room on your hands and knees sobbing. Because that has no effect either. I've tried it.

So how do you use your body language to your advantage? Well, Amy Cuddy's studies are amongst many that reach the conclusion that our body language influences how other people perceive us. Striding purposefully into a room to deliver an important presentation gives you an air of confidence that the butterflies in your stomach might possibly belie.

Fortunately, nobody can see the butterflies, just the confident stride.

But what if you simply mimic the mannerisms and gestures of someone that you want to get to like you, such as a new client or colleague? Will it work?

You don't decide on how you wish to be seen but, rather, you just copy?

Displaying a degree of empathy with a potential client can obviously help to bolster a relationship. But is it as simple as copying a hand gesture, a particular way of standing or sitting, or a distinctive nod of the head?

Well, there is evidence to suggest that subtle mimicking of another person's body language can increase their liking of you. For many years, Bush and Blair were as thick as thieves. Or, should I say, enjoyed a 'special relationship'. They both developed a style of public speaking that was almost identical. It would start with dramatic pauses and simple hand gestures, continue with subtle arm movements and then often conclude with the invasion of a small country. Coincidence? I think not.

You may well have noticed it with your friends in a social situation where everyone stands or everyone sits down. We naturally want to be like the other person and subconsciously reflect their body language. Or they ours. Observe friends having a drink and you'll notice that they tend to actually put the cup or the glass to their lips at the same time. Cyclists, runners, rowers enjoy doing the same thing at the same time – all part of the need to belong.

But if you're still a little sceptical, here's the proof. Psychologists John Chartrand and Tanya Bargh of New York University carried out a series of experiments to determine whether mimicking another person's habits really does influence how much they like you. Testing what they called 'the chameleon effect', they divided up their sample of guinea pigs into two groups. Each group spent 20 minutes or so chatting to a member of the researchers' team whom they had never met before. One group of researchers was instructed to subtly mimic the person's body language, such as folding their arms, scratching their nose, tapping the arm rest, waggling their foot – any little nuance that they could mimic without being rumbled. Meanwhile, the researchers in the control group sat quite still throughout their conversation and didn't attempt to mimic any body language at all.

Afterwards the participants were asked to provide a mark out of 10 to indicate how much they liked the person they had been talking to and how well they had got on with each other. The results supported the theory that mimicking a person's body language does, indeed, increase their liking of you, with the group whose actions were imitated consistently giving higher scores than those whose body language wasn't mimicked in any way.

In the real world, of course, it should be a little more natural. If you literally mimic and imitate someone's every movement it looks like you've been on a course. It looks like you're trying too hard. If you copy these traits at exactly the same time as the other person is doing them it would give the game away. They would probably start to shuffle uneasily in their chair and look at you askance. And when you do likewise, they may even begin to sweat a little. And if you can replicate that, you'll soon find yourself being frog-marched off the premises, whilst screaming to the security guards 'Keep in step, boys'. That would be taking it too far.

So try the 'chameleon effect' yourself the next time you meet someone new you want to impress and get to like you. But gently, be careful not to overdo it. Because if they've also read this chapter you may find yourself acting out a bizarre Laurel and Hardy routine.

8

How your behaviours dictate either successful long-term partnerships – Or relationships heading for disaster

The Holmes and Rahe Stress Scale is a well-recognized method of measuring stress in our lives. The number of 'Life Change Units' that apply to events in the past year of an individual's life are added and the final score gives a rough estimate of how stress affects health. The need to be in a happy relationship where we feel loved, important and part of something – to belong – shows up very clearly when we look at the worst things that can happen in someone's life. Top of the stress list is death of a spouse and divorce and marital separation come second and third. Of the top 20, 11 are about relationships and only 2 are about money.

So, for over 40 years, the psychologist, Professor John Gottman, has devoted his life to analysing the relationships of married couples.

During that time, he's closely observed couples in an effort to understand what kind of behaviours predict either a successful long-term partnership, or a marriage destined for divorce. If you ever wake up and there's a man at the end of your bed taking notes, it's probably John. He'll flash you his ID and be on his way. If he flashes anything else, call the police.

Although a lot of Gottman's work has been on traditional couples, he – and others – have found that the principles, techniques and signals are the same across all relationships and apply to the business world too. Selling in business to business is usually all about relationships, after all. So here, courtesy of Gottman, are the four main signs that he's identified as being particularly unhealthy in any kind of partnership.

1. **Criticism**
   Everyone complains to each other from time to time. And ironically it's the people we see most of both at work and at home that we complain to (and about) the most. But it's a particular type of corrosive criticism that Gottman identifies as being so destructive. Anything that involves a frying pan, for instance. Or, more specifically, when the criticism strikes at the very core of the other person's being, their personality. For example: 'You're late because you don't care about me.'

   Anyone can be late, of course, but here the criticism implies that you did it on purpose or for some other deeper, sinister meaning. According to John, repeated criticisms of this nature mean that the end of the relationship is close at hand. A bit like the frying pan.

2. Contempt

In couples' relationships, Gottman found that contempt for a partner was the single greatest predictor of divorce. It can involve sarcasm, name-calling, mimicking and eye-rolling.

Whatever form it takes, contempt makes the other person feel worthless. It cuts across the first three fundamental psychological drivers.

It's also bad for your health. Gottman found that couples who were contemptuous of each other often suffered more infectious diseases like colds and flu.

Which is why he always took an extra pace back from the bed.

If you have contempt for someone at work it will show. If you send an email about someone at work it's best to assume they will see the email even if you don't send it to them. You can always deny you said it but you can't retract what you write.

3. Defensiveness

A person is too defensive when they are constantly making excuses for their failures or slip-ups. Sure, we all do it, but when it becomes a persistent theme it often signals the end of a relationship. Worse still is when defensiveness is coupled with trying to score points off the other person. Not like in squash or badminton – that's just tactics. But in a personal or trusting business relationship you're supposed to support one another. After all, life is difficult enough without being attacked from within.

4. Stonewalling

Stonewalling is when a person metaphorically raises the drawbridge and cuts off all communication. There are no nods of encouragement when their partner speaks, no attempt to empathize and no effort to respond or connect. Hence the phrase: 'It's like talking to a brick wall.'

Stonewalling is often a result of a prolonged period of criticism, contempt and defensiveness. For some people, the only response to this worsening situation is to shut up shop and send the other person to Coventry.

Note: you don't have to be a retailer in the West Midlands to practise this.

So there you have it. Or, hopefully, you don't. But if you do happen to spot any of the above signs creeping into your relationships then it's a good idea to do something about it before it's too late.

So what CAN you do if those four things exist in any of your relationships?

Well, Gottman has found happy couples use five times more positive behaviours in their arguments than negative ones. And of course, this applies to any type of relationship. For instance, humour is a good way to break the tension of an argument.

Just don't use what might be perceived to be insulting or hurtful terms, even in a playful manner, unless you know that person very well indeed. I saw one exchange at a coffee break between two ladies who had told me prior to the conference that they were helping each other lose weight. They had agreed they would support each other and knew each other's target weights. But when one said to the other 'Steady on the chocolate buns' as she was reaching for said bun, the expression 'if looks could kill' took on a whole new meaning. She meant it as a joke to her friend, but another dozen people were in earshot and her friend was mightily offended. It's the difference between intent and impact. What you mean as a jokey aside can easily be taken the wrong way.

Here are Gottman's top four tips:

1. **Edit yourself**
   Don't say out loud every critical thought you have whilst discussing a touchy topic. Much better to just think it. Remember, everything you say to the other person will either nurture your relationship or tear it down. You may win the argument but lose the rapport.

2. **Soften your 'start up'**
   Bring up problems gently and without blame rather than kicking off with a critical or contemptuous remark. There's plenty of time for those later. If you have a long-standing poor relationship with someone at work but you need to liaise with that person on a regular basis, ask if you can buy them a coffee at a neutral venue. Better still, go for a walk with them. Tell them

about the positives first. Talk about how everyone would benefit if you could do something to improve the relationship. Listen carefully and ask them what they would like in an ideal world before you have your say.

3. **Accept influence from the other person.**
In heterosexual marriages, Gottman discovered that a relationship succeeds to the extent that the husband can accept influence from his wife. So if you're a bloke, man up and do as you're told. The good news is that women are already well practised at accepting influence from men.

We all want to be important. And that means we all want to be heard. And THAT means you have to accept influence from the other person.

4. **Learn to repair and exit the argument**
Give in when the other person wants something from you that doesn't mean that much to you. In all relationships, you often have to yield to win, much like in the martial art of Aikido. Not to be confused with Tai Kwando where you just beat the crap out of each other. Don't be afraid to give ground, back down and 'tackle the problem together'.

The most successful relationships are those where each person refuses to accept hurtful behaviour from the other. Plus, when discussing problems, as Gottman says, they make five times as many positive statements as negative ones. For example, 'We laugh a lot at work' as opposed to 'We never have any fun in the office'.

Remember, relationships are only successful to the degree that the problems you have are ones you can cope with. And what really matters is not conflict resolution, but the attitudes that surround discussion of the conflict. Good relationships develop when the people in the relationship have the ability to exchange viewpoints and accept that there will always be differences between them.

And, of course, the relationships we have with our children can affect them for the rest of their lives. Young people who, through no fault of their own, have an absent parent or, indeed, one in prison can feel that they too are serving a sentence.

According to Professor Bruce Robinson, who is based at the Sir Charles Gairdner hospital in Perth, WA, the absence of a strong father figure increases the chances of a child taking drugs and suffering from depression dramatically. When a parent is imprisoned they leave a life behind on the outside; a life that includes a spouse and children; a family that has to try and rebuild, often shorn of their main breadwinner or primary carer, not to mention the love and support of a mum or dad.

Two thirds of boys with a father in prison go on to offend themselves.

Why is that? The availability bias? A role model with no moral compass? Or is it that having a father taken away from a young child and put in prison cuts right across all the seven psychological drivers?

The child no longer has the love from the father, feels he or she is not important to the father, no longer has the sense of belonging to the family unit they enjoyed, has lost a belief in the father, has too much uncertainty, doesn't grow and learn from the father and the father is no longer in the 'place' that that child knows as home.

And there is one other factor that is important to a child growing up and helping any relationship. The most successful couples say 'please' and 'thank you'. A good parent treats a child like an adult and doesn't assume the child will do as they are told. They say 'please' and 'thank you'. Saying 'please' and 'thank you' makes people feel loved and important.

In the 70s, Abba thanked us for the music. In the 60s, Frank Sinatra thanked us for the memories.

And in the 1958 musical *Gigi*, Maurice Chevalier thanked heaven for little girls. I believe he's still helping police with their enquiries.

Like me, you were no doubt taught as a kid that good manners cost nothing. We learned that saying 'please' and 'thank you' was a common courtesy that we afforded to others and hoped to get back in return. But what they didn't tell us was that they have a very real value too. You see, recent scientific evidence suggest that saying 'please' and 'thank you' can actually help us to influence the behaviour of others.

Research teams led by Adam Grant and Francesco Gino of the Universities of Pennsylvania and North Carolina, respectively, conducted studies to prove that saying 'thank you' has a genuine benefit to both parties. It's been known for some time that showing gratitude improves a person's physical health and produces positive emotional states. This could be the reason why contestants on *The Apprentice* always say 'Thank you, Lord Sugar' (so much better than 'Thank You Sralan' don't you think?) immediately after he tells them they're fired. Why else would they thank him?

However, Grant and Gino wanted to discover what effect showing gratitude had on the person being thanked; the thankee, as it were. In particular, they wanted to find out whether it motivated them in some way, or just made them feel good. In the first study, 69 participants were each sent a letter by a fictitious student called Eric. (I know what you're thinking. I didn't go to Uni with anyone called Eric either, but they didn't smell a rat.) Accompanying it was a note explaining that it was the first draft of a covering letter for a job application and politely asked them to provide some feedback on its merits.

Those who replied each got a second letter from Eric, requesting more help with another cover letter. However, this time, half of them got a politely worded communiqué thanking them for their help so far, whilst half got a 'neutral' reply that gave no thanks at all. As expected, this difference in wording had a marked effect on how willing people were to help Eric further. Only 32% of those who received the 'no thanks' letter provided more feedback. However, a mighty 66% of the other group were happy to provide feedback to his second letter. In short, his 'thanks' had more than doubled the response rate.

So why is this?

Naturally, Eric's gratitude made people feel good about themselves and boosted their self-esteem. But researchers discovered that the real motivating factor was that they appreciated being needed and felt more socially valued when thanked. This feeling of social worth helps people get over the factors that stop us from helping others. For instance, when we see an elderly person struggling to cross a road, we're often unsure whether or not to provide assistance. They might not appreciate it; they might be too proud. But when you do help them and they thank you it motivates you to do the same for others. Even if they don't want to go. Only yesterday I shepherded a dozen frail pensioners to a traffic island on a dual carriageway before dashing off for a train. Looking back, I was perhaps a little over eager to help.

To find out whether Eric's thanks would make people more likely to help a different person, the researchers conducted a second study. A day after Eric's letter arrived, an email was sent to the participants from 'Steven' asking for similar help. This time only 25% of those who had received no thanks from Eric decided to help Steven, whilst 55% of those who had received gratitude duly obliged. Proof that the boost to a person's social worth carries over from one day to the next and from one person to the next.

For most of us, expressing our thanks is an everyday occurrence that we take for granted. But psychologically it has a very important role to play for both the person giving and the person receiving. All these studies reveal that gratitude is more than just a social nicety, or a way of making the helper feel good; it reassures others that their help was actually appreciated and it encourages further prosocial behaviour.

So, in summary, don't say out loud every critical thought you have whilst discussing a touchy topic with someone. If you have a problem with someone, ask for time with them, begin gently and without blame. Learn to repair and exit the argument. Accept influence from the other person. It's got to be give and take in the long term. And finally, keep focusing on the positives and never underestimate the power of saying 'thank you' and showing how grateful you are.

9
Why persistence pays when asking for a favour

When requesting a favour from someone, if at first they don't say 'yes' simply ask again.

It may sound like an unsophisticated approach, but statistics prove that it pays to be persistent when asking someone for a favour. That's what Professor Franklin Boster of Michigan State University discovered in his experiment on the subject. He concluded that if your request for a favour is refused, you simply ask the question 'Why not?' and then deal with the objections.

However, according to Boster, the key lies in your ability to transform the 'no' from a flat refusal into merely an obstacle to be overcome. The theory goes that if you can deal with the obstacle, your request is more likely to be granted. To see how well this simple approach worked, Boster tested it against three other well-established methods of gaining compliance to a request. They are:

Rejection and Retreat
Here, you first make a very large request which is easily turned down; the metaphorical door being slammed in

your face. But then you follow up straight away with a much smaller request which now, by comparison, looks very reasonable. This is proven to substantially increase compliance.

Foot in the door

This is the exact reverse of 'Rejection and Retreat'. First you ask for something small, then crank it up. The theory goes that agreeing to the smaller request makes people more likely to agree to a second, larger one. The art is in judging the step up just right. 'Actually, make mine a double' is a good example of this.

Placebo Information

This is when you give someone a very poor reason to comply. In a now famous study, Harvard University psychologist Ellen Langer asked three different variations of a single request to people using a photocopier.

First, she asked 'Excuse me, I have five pages. May I use the Xerox machine?' and 60% allowed her to go ahead of them.

When Langer was more specific and asked, 'Excuse me, I have five pages. May I use the Xerox machine because I'm in a rush?' the rate of compliance shot up to 94%.

And in the third request: 'Excuse me, I have five pages. May I use the Xerox machine because I have to make some copies?' the rate of compliance stayed about the same – at 93% — when the excuse was completely ridiculous – a 'placebo request'.

Everyone in the queue needed to make copies, but Langer was able to jump the queue by simply providing an excuse in the first place. It was the presence of the word 'because' that made it easier for her to skip the wait. However, it rarely works in court with smart people. 'I'm sorry I was speeding your Worship but I was going too fast to read the signs' probably wouldn't work.

Anyway, to test all these methods, Boster asked 60 random passers-by if they would be kind enough to look after a bicycle for 10 minutes: 20% of people who were subject to the 'Rejection and Retreat' method complied with the request, whilst 45% responded positively to the 'Placebo Information' approach. However, trumping both these methods was the 'Why Not?' approach which scored an impressive 60% compliance rating. Which possibly just goes to prove that most people can't think quick enough on their feet.

I'm currently looking after three bicycles and a sheep dog.

Of course, if you have small children you will know about the power of persistent questioning. Repeated requests give the impression of urgency and probably trigger a person's feelings of either guilt or sympathy. However, my favourite explanation is to do with cognitive dissonance. This is the term psychologists give to the behaviour whereby we try to avoid inconsistencies in our thinking that cause us mental anguish. For example, it feels dissonant – the two ideas butting up against each other – not to comply after objections have been effectively dealt with. After all, if there's no reason not to do it, why not do it?

These techniques may well be even more powerful when used together. Especially since the term 'Why not?' can be tagged onto almost anything. The only down side of the 'Why not?' approach is that it requires the wit to dispel objections. But then again, anticipating objections is a standard part of negotiation, so many of these can be prepared in advance.

It might feel cheeky to keep asking 'Why not?' when people refuse, but this experiment suggests it can be a powerful way to encourage compliance.

But what if that still doesn't work? You've asked someone to do something for you and they just say 'no'?

Well, here's the good news.

Although everybody gets rejection and we all get down, after a while a funny thing happens. We don't feel quite so bad.

Why is that?

Did you read about the guy who mistakenly threw away a £100,000 winning scratch card? Naturally, he was gutted at the time. But now he's probably having a really good laugh about it.

Or maybe not.

However, for most of us, bad news often turns out to be nothing like as devastating as we first feared. Why is that? Well, a study by Daniel Gilbert at Harvard University gives us a clue. He set up a series of classic social psychology studies on experiences that most people would be familiar with, including going for a job interview and getting rejected. Of course, as with all these experiments, things weren't quite what they seemed. Firstly, all the interviewees were led to believe there was an actual job on offer. Then they were asked to complete a questionnaire which included a section about how they would feel if they didn't get it. To quantify their disappointment they were asked to predict the change in their mood on a scale of 1 to 10 where 10 was happy at getting the job. All agreed that their mood would worsen by two points to eight if they were rejected.

Naturally, nobody was offered the job. What Gilbert was interested in was their *reaction* to the bad news, and in particular, how this differed from their prediction. But there was another little twist in the tail. Half the group was interviewed by just one person, and half by a panel of three. This made it easier for those rejected by one person to rationalize the decision as just one person's preferences. But for those who were rejected by three people it was naturally more difficult to dismiss, since this was seemingly a considered judgement by a panel.

Immediately after the rejection, those interviewed by just one person could rationalize the decision. Their good mood fell appreciably less than that of those rejected by the panel of three, and none of them had their mood drop as low as they had predicted.

On being told that it was all an experiment and there was never any job on offer, one woman overturned the desk, set fire to the curtains, and stormed out.

It happens.

Fact is we all have an inbuilt psychological immune system that recalibrates the world and our feelings. So whenever life kicks us in the unmentionables, the psychological immune system gets to work rationalizing what's happened and, over time, stops it hurting as much as we feared. We don't want too much inconsistency so the brain recalibrates.

So don't live in fear of how you will feel at bad news. Go ask that someone to do something for you even if you think you have little chance of them doing it.

Why not?

If you are rejected you won't feel as bad as you think anyway.

Often, though, there's more to it than simply asking again. Fact is, if you are genuinely able to see the argument against your proposition you're then more prepared to counter it. You see, research has shown that if you present both sides of an argument, you are far more likely to persuade your audience to your way of thinking than if you simply present them with your idea or proposal. It suggests that you've considered the alternative. You've weighed up all the facts. You've arrived at the correct decision.

To only give one side of the argument makes people feel unimportant – that you haven't considered the options because you thought it wasn't worth it. *You* may be certain of the pros and cons, but they want to see that you have balanced certainty and uncertainty by studying the plusses and minuses and carefully concluded that there is a clear 'winner'.

Expressions like 'One of the benefits of x is that … but the flip side of the coin is …'.

Even better, expressions like 'I think there is some merit in x but there is a lot to be said for y and I value your views. Perhaps together we can come to a better decision?'

It's no coincidence that politicians spend half their time telling you where the opposition went wrong before suggesting what they're going to do. They don't introduce policies simply to 'make things better' but to 'put things right'. The implication being that the alternative was a mistake.

It's the same with *The X Factor*. Simon Cowell will often announce that what he just heard was the worst ever rendition of a particular song and that the wannabe superstar has no talent whatsoever. This will be delivered against a backdrop of boos and catcalls suggesting that the audience may disagree. However, Louis Walsh will take a more pragmatic view. He'll tell us that they were brave to choose such a difficult song. He'll continue with some reference to them 'giving it their all' and may even highlight a moment where they were actually in tune. But then he'll reflect that sadly, on balance, they're probably not quite ready for stardom just yet. Same conclusion, but expressed in a more reasoned way. And we've stopped throwing things at the television.

So when presenting any kind of proposition, remember that there's always two sides to an argument. Work out what that other side is and be prepared to argue for it as well as against it. Don't do all this in a dismissive manner but in a way that suggests you've given it due consideration. Don't be afraid to highlight the benefits of the counter-argument. After all, these are the qualities that people who *do* hold this view will put forward in its favour. But then go on to describe the pitfalls of such an approach. This strengthens your own argument and lends it credibility.

Psychologically the other person feels like you are being more honest with them and that they are part of the decision-making process – that they 'belong' to this cabal that will make the final judgement. You are making them feel more important and that you need their opinion.

But don't take my word for it. Daniel O' Keefe at the University of Illinois collated the results of more than 100 studies on the subject conducted over a 50-year period. Twenty thousand people took part in the research, which saw psychologists compare one-sided and two-sided arguments to see which were the most persuasive in different contexts and with a variety of audiences. It was concluded beyond doubt that two-sided arguments are more persuasive than their one-sided equivalents.

So present both sides of an argument when you are trying to win someone over to show them that you've considered the alternatives. And ideally have one of the options as a very large request which can easily be turned down. You are much more likely to be convincing. And they'll think they made the decision.

And if they say no, ask again ...

10

The power of belief and the 'illusory correlation'

Thomas Gilovich is Professor of Psychology at Cornell University. He's spent a lifetime researching 'behavioural economics'.

In a survey he conducted amongst high school seniors in the USA, he and his colleagues found that 70% of the students thought they were above average in leadership ability and only 2% thought they were below average. In terms of ability to get along with others, all students thought they were above average, 60% thought they were in the top 10% and 25% thought they were in the top 1%.

Kids eh?

But in another survey 94% of university professors believed they were better at their job than their colleagues.

So it's not just young students.

Most people think they are better than average. You probably do too. And by definition, that must mean that most people think they are better than most. It's all part of being important. The question is, does it matter? Is self-deception a good or bad thing in the workplace?

Stanford University psychologists Amos Tversky and George Quattrone conducted a classic social psychology experiment to study self-deception. As you're getting to know now about such experiments, the researchers lied to the participants about every aspect of the study. Firstly, they told them the study was about the 'psychological and medical aspects of athletics'. Then they tricked them into believing that a measure of good health could be gauged by the length of time you could submerge your arms in very cold water.

Naturally, this was nonsense. All it showed was how ready they were to deceive themselves and what they would do for 50 quid. Typically most people could endure the cold water for about 30 seconds. To make participants believe the study was real they were given other tasks to do as well. Walking over hot coals with no shoes on wasn't one of them but it would have made an interesting foot note. Instead, they did a stint on an exercise bike.

Crucially, they were then given a short lecture about how life expectancy depended on your type of heart. Lying through their teeth, and presumably just managing to suppress a giggle, the researchers revealed that there were two types of heart: one associated with poor health and one associated with top class athletes.

Continuing with the porkies, the researchers then said it was possible to tell which type of heart you had by measuring your tolerance to cold water after exercise. They'd just worked up a sweat on the bikes, remember. But here's the rub. One half were told that an *increased* tolerance to cold water indicated a strong heart, whilst the other half were told that it was a *decreased* tolerance to cold water.

You can probably guess the outcome. For the first half who were told that cold tolerance is healthy, subjects were able to submerge their arms in cold water much longer the second time compared to the first time. At first, they averaged at 35 seconds but during the second attempt, they lasted longer than 45 seconds.

On the contrary, the other half who were told that cold tolerance was *unhealthy*, correspondingly lessened their submersion time by about 10 seconds.

So, when people thought a higher cold tolerance meant a healthier heart, they held their arms underwater much longer; and those who believed the reverse did otherwise and felt they could no longer tolerate the cold.

Once people believed that an increased or decreased tolerance to cold water indicated a strong heart they acted accordingly. The power of belief.

To further test whether subjects were self-deceiving, they were asked whether they intentionally held their arms underwater longer or shorter as it indicates the health of their heart. Among the 38 subjects, 29 denied they did and 9 confessed indirectly. (Those nine justified that the water had changed temperature, thus explaining the change, but of course the water had the same temperature all throughout the experiment.)

They were then asked whether they really did believe that they had a healthy heart or not. More than half of the subjects that denied intentionally holding their arms underwater for a longer or shorter period thought they had the healthier type of heart. While among the nine confessors, only 20% thought they had the healthier heart. This only means that the deniers were more likely to be really deceiving themselves because they thought that the test was really telling them that they had a healthy heart.

Obviously, submerging your arms for more or less time in cold water is not diagnostic of whether you have a healthy heart and you can't cause a change in your heart's type.

But the subjects behaved as if they could actually change their heart type. Everybody deceived themselves into believing that they had an athlete's heart by either enduring the cold water for less or more time than previously – depending upon the lie they were told. One man was determined to deceive himself so much he submerged his whole head into the water for three minutes and then called for the hot coals 'for good measure' as he was led away to the ambulance.

Or did I just make that up?

No matter. What this study suggests is that for many people self-deception is easy. So, if you manage people, why not tell them they are very, very, good indeed? Because the more they believe, the better they'll be.

And if they are actually lying rather than just experiencing self-deception, how can you tell?

Well, firstly, the beauty of always being honest is that you don't have to recall what you said to someone. Whereas whenever you lie, you *always* have to remember in case you're asked again. There are the deceitful whoppers often designed to save a bit of money, or get you out of a tight spot, and the little white lies usually told simply to save someone's feelings. For example, '*No, of course, your bottom doesn't look big in that*' is more likely to precede a successful evening than if your answer includes a reference to say, a baboon or a sumo wrestler.

The truth is, lies are very difficult to detect. Even the classically studied tell-tale signs are no real indicator. Today, those experienced and well-practised in lying rarely fidget or look away when they're not telling the truth. They don't scratch the back of their neck, act nervously, or change the pitch of their voice. If they touch their nose it's probably itching. If they touch yours, you're standing too close.

So how do you tell? Well, years of researching real police interviews allowed Professor Aldert Vrij of the University of Portsmouth to provide some guidance about what non-verbal signals represent. Firstly, it's important to consider a person's natural behaviour. A friendly, gregarious outgoing character who turns up on your doorstep asking to borrow an axe is more likely to get assistance than someone who's a dead ringer for Hannibal Lecter. Similarly, introverts or socially nervous people sometimes give the false impression that they're lying. But they're not.

Researchers concluded that the way to spot a lie is to study someone's behaviour when they are telling the truth, and then to compare this with their behaviour when suspected of lying. Lying places high cognitive demands on an individual and the more awkward the questions asked, the more pressure they feel, and the more physical signs they display. This is basically how a lie detector works, highlighting the difference in things like facial movements, heart rate and sweat glands.

Fact is, you often don't have long to spot the liar. Not only is it just in micro-expressions, but they last less than a second. Micro-expressions are facial expressions that flash on someone's face for a fraction of a second and reveal the person's true emotion, underneath the lie. Some people may be naturally sensitive to them, but almost anybody can train themselves to detect these micro-expressions. The eyebrows being drawn upwards towards the middle of the fore-head, causing short lines to appear across the skin of the forehead are one give away. Eyebrows suddenly moving down and a quick movement of the head backwards usually mean they think it's *you* that's lying.

The real key though is in the person's eye movements. You can usually tell if a person is remembering something or making something up based on eye movements.

There is one theory that when people are remembering details, their eyes move up and to the left if they are right handed. And if they are lying they look to the right as they are making the story up. The reverse is true of left-handed people.

But even if this is true it's very difficult to spot and remember whether the person is left or right handed. I have a friend who plays golf right handed and putts left handed. I have a son who writes left handed and does everything else right handed.

But the eyes can be a sign – particularly if you bear in mind Aldert Vrij's advice to compare them to a person's natural behaviour. People tend to either blink more rapidly as they're telling a lie or don't blink at all. But be careful about assessing the truthfulness of someone's statement based on eye movements alone. Recent scientific studies have cast doubt on the idea that looking in a certain direction can help pinpoint someone who is lying. Many scientists believe that eye directionality is a statistically poor indicator of truthfulness.

Of course, if you have a meeting with a Sales Director and you need to know his *real* plans for next year, it's probably not the done thing to wire him up first. So here's a tip. Rely on your intuition. If you're a salesperson it will doubtlessly be finely honed any way. If you're in a meeting and something doesn't quite *feel* right it probably means that something *isn't* quite right. Either that or your underwear is on back to front.

In a nutshell, implicit or broadly unconscious processes can be more effective at detecting a lie than conscious directed thought. It's a big nutshell, granted. So if you want to be sure of the truth, ask someone to recount the story over and over again. And don't forget to look out for the TNTs – Tiny Noticeable Things – that are different, as well as any discrepancies in the answer. As they say on the television, the truth is out there.

And finally, in this chapter on 'illusory correlation' and the strange beliefs we hold on connections, it's worth looking at a study into the remuneration packages of top CEOs, which suggests that there's a direct correlation between the size of their salary and their prowess on the golf course.

Two Spanish academics studied the relationship between salaries of golf-playing CEOs versus their non-playing counterparts. Despite having the unlikely sounding Spanish names of Gueorgui Kolev and Robin Hogarth I've decided to give them the benefit of the doubt and share their findings. Gueorgui and Robin – or the Caped Crusader and the Boy Wonder as I like to call them – discovered not only a direct correlation between the size of a CEO's salary and their inclination to play golf, but as their golfing ability improved, so too did their wage packet. What's more, non-golfing CEOs were, on average, the lowest paid of all.

I call it the 'Play and Pay' effect, since the more top executives play, the more they seem to get paid. I know green fees can be expensive, but there's got to be more to it than that.

But here's the rub. The rub of the green, you might say. The antithetical irony (look it up, I did) was that the better the CEOs were at golf, the worse their shares performed. Presumably because they spent far more time on the golf course than in the boardroom. But why should someone get paid more when their per- formance actually deteriorates?

Well, it seems that in many people's minds, being good at sport suggests that you are also good at many other things too. Like running a multinational corporation.

Even if it's just running it into the ground.

This state of affairs is what psychologists call an 'illusory correlation'. After many gruelling hours spent on the golf course, Gueorgui and Robin concluded that 'illusionary correlation' is a powerful influencer in big business and the only reason that they could see why golf-playing CEOs were so handsomely rewarded – even when their company wasn't doing particularly well.

Designer clothing is another case in point. Research confirms that it's not the design itself that counts, but rather the label. And who better to prove this theory than those European style icons with their bright orange trousers, the Dutch. Okay, so maybe the Italians or the French would have been better, but it was Rob Nelissen and Marijn Meijers of Tilburg University in the Netherlands who got there first.

Their pioneering work studied the effect of wearing designer labels in a variety of situations. For instance, when collecting money for charity, being recommended for a job, or simply seeking cooperation from another person. They discovered that wearing designer labels made people more likely to react positively to your request than when wearing normal, non-designer labels.

To prove the point, volunteers were shown a picture of the same man and asked to rate him from 1 to 5 in terms of his wealth and status. The only difference between the pictures was the branding on his polo shirt. Those who were shown a picture of him in a Lacoste or Tommy Hilfiger shirt rated him around 3.5, whilst those who saw the same man in a non-designer shirt rated him just 2.9. The bad news for Slazenger is that they fared even worse than wearing no logo at all.

Ouch!

The illusory correlation extended to a female researcher who wore a sweater with a designer logo, then next, an identical sweater with no logo. Some 52% of people agreed to take a 'consumer survey' in a shopping mall when faced with the Tommy Hilfiger label, compared with only 13% who saw no logo.

So why do labels count so much? According to Nelissen and Meijers it's the same reason that the peacock with the best tail gets the peahens. People react to designer labels as signals of underlying quality. And they assume that only the best can afford them.

It's a belief they have. And once they believe that a brand is expensive and only the rich can afford it, they assume anyone buying that brand is rich. And if they believe that Slazenger is a poor brand, then someone wearing it is of low wealth and status.

It's no coincidence that the most prestigious brands in the world – like Louis Vuitton, Hermes and

Rolex – are very particular about how their brands are portrayed. Every little detail matters. They are totally focused on everything that is said and seen about their brands being just as they would want it to be.

And that's why people will willingly buy counterfeit goods if they bear the right label. It's the little logo that says everything and is so influential. Mind you, if you get stopped at customs with a suitcase full of them, you'll probably need a lawyer too.

But why do people buy the real thing when they know they can buy a 'genuine fake' and no one would know?

Because THEY know. It's how the brand makes you FEEL that really matters.

The bottom line? Designer logos work. Just make sure you're wearing the right one.

Of course, there are lots of other 'illusionary correlations' that people *believe* to be a true indicator. Like the size of a man's shoes and the size of his manhood. Or indeed, the type of car that he drives. In many respects it's just 'learned behaviour'. When we form our views we like to think that we are rational and logical, but one of our drivers is to believe and we form beliefs very quickly. It somehow insults our own intelligence to not form a view.

But many of these beliefs are wrong and many of them are just superstitions. There are footballers who won't put their shirt on until the pitch is in sight. If a woman is being interviewed for jobs and she believes she gets a better response from potential employers when she wears a specific pair of earrings, she'll wear those earrings to every interview.

I'm no different. After once winning a big finance account against all the odds, I always wore the same lucky tie in subsequent major pitches to finance clients. Although, at my colleagues' request, I did put a stop to running around the room with my shirt pulled over my head. That was undignified and I've never done it since.

So, is this behaviour irrational nonsense or does it actually work by giving us more confidence and self-belief? Well, let's go back to golf again and a study by German psychologist Lysann Damisch. He wanted to test the theory that simple superstitions, like using a lucky charm, or some other 'illusory correlation', improve performance on both motor and mental tasks.

In the first experiment, Damisch asked a number of golfers to have a go at holing a 1-metre putt. It should be straightforward but, of course, many missed. However, when he repeated the experiment on another hole, again from 1 metre, the number of successful putts increased by 33%. Why? Because this time he handed each golfer his 'lucky ball'. And with that, more of them simply believed they would hole the putt.

Damisch repeated the experiment twice more in studies that tested both memory and puzzle-solving abilities. Again – fingers crossed – the results were markedly improved when the participant was given a 'lucky charm' as part of the experiment. The researchers concluded that these superstitions improved performance because they gave people the confidence to aim higher and keep trying.

So it seems that believing in superstition helps to relieve nervous tension and allows us the illusion of control in what is sometimes a scary, random world.

And as for the direct correlation between the size of a CEO's salary and their ability to play golf? Well, I'll leave it up to you to decide whether or not there's anything in it and you should either take up the game or improve if you already play. However, that old maxim 'If you want to get ahead, get a hat' does seem to ring true in the business world – so long as it's a golfing hat.

In the introduction we talked about the fourth 'driver' being this need we all have to 'believe'. In this chapter we have explored why it is that most people think they are better than average and how, if people believe that an increased or decreased tolerance to cold water indicates a strong heart, they will act accordingly in an experiment and prove to themselves they have a strong heart.

So how does this knowledge help you to influence someone when they have a strong belief? Well, the first thing to recognize is that a firmly held belief is not easily changed. You have to ask lots of questions and ask how they have arrived at that view. Ask for the evidence that supports the view. And don't be critical even if you know you are right and they are wrong.

Now, if you'll excuse me, I've got to wear my lucky golf glove, nip down to Pannal Golf Club in my Lexus LS460 and do a bit of business. Just as soon as I've found my size 12 golf shoes, that is.

11

The anchor effect, the drive we have for 'more' and how to improve your negotiating skills

You may not have heard of the anchoring effect when negotiating.

But you'll certainly have experienced it.

To illustrate the anchoring effect, let's say I ask 200 people how old Mahatma Gandhi was when he died.

For half of the 200 I preface the question by saying: 'Did he die before or after the age of 9?' For the other half I say: 'Did he die before or after the age of 140?'

Obviously these are not very helpful statements. Anyone who has any clue who Gandhi was will know that he was definitely older than 9 when he died; while the oldest person who ever lived was 122. So why bother making these apparently stupid statements?

Because, according to the results of a study conducted by Fritz Strack and Thomas Mussweiler of the University of Würzburg, these initial statements, despite being unhelpful, affect the estimates people make.

In their experiment, the first group guessed an average age of 50 and the second, 67.

Neither was that close, he was actually assassinated at 78, but you can still see the effect of the initial number.

The anchor state.

Dan Ariely of Duke University and two colleagues, MIT's Drazen Prelec and Carnegie Mellon economist George Loewenstein, got a group of campus volunteers into a room and showed each volunteer one of several products: a cordless keyboard computer, a video game and a bottle of wine. The subjects were then offered the opportunity to buy the item at a price equal to the last two digits of their Social Security numbers – obviously a random price. Additionally, they were each asked the maximum price they would be willing to pay.

What the research revealed was that the maximum price the subjects assigned was driven largely by the random offer they had received only moments before. Those with high Social Security numbers systematically bid more than those with low ones. Because they didn't have a clue about what the merchandise was worth to them, they were vulnerable to suggestion and manipulation.

These might seem like silly little experiments that psychologists do to try and suggest that people can be influenced without them knowing, but actually it's showing us something fundamental about the way we think. It's so basic to how we experience the world that we often don't notice it.

You can see the same effect in salary negotiations. There's some evidence that when the initial anchor figure is set high, the final negotiated amount will usually be higher. It's all about the initial benchmark which then influences the final outcome in your favour.

You'll have taken part in such benchmarking exercises if you've ever haggled in a souk. The seller demands 100 units of the local currency and you counter this by offering just 30. He comes down a little, you go up a little, and eventually you settle on 50. A great deal for you since you got that delightful stuffed camel for half the asking price and didn't even have to throw in your new shirt. However, his asking price of 100 was probably ten times more than he was willing to accept. So you actually paid five times more than necessary.

Anchored.

He set it, so he was always going to win.

But the seller understands this drive we have for 'more'. He makes you feel important as he seems to treat you as an individual. We all feel better if we think we have got a great deal. This example illustrates something else fundamental about the way we think. Every day we use anchors or reference points to make decisions and evaluations. If you're an estate agent, car salesperson or negotiator of any sort you'll probably be nodding your head right now. If you're a nodding dog in a used car you'll probably be doing the same. Not particularly relevant to the story; it's just what they do. I thought I'd mention it.

Anyway, establishing anchors is a vital step in the negotiating process for any salesperson. It defines the ballpark. And, whether we like it not, the whole negotiating process will be influenced by whatever that starting figure is. It's a technique also known as 'Rejection and Retreat' since the buyer always has the option to walk away from the deal at any time. But if they really want what you've got to sell, the chances are they'll stay and negotiate.

As a seller, that usually means starting at the highest price you think you can get. That's why car sticker prices on garage forecourts are high. The dealer will always accept less, but it's up to you to negotiate them down. The same goes for salary reviews. You might hope for a £2,000 rise, but unless you ask for more than this there's little chance of getting it. Particularly if your employer opens the negotiations by suggesting just £1,000. In that instance, getting £1,500 feels like a result and both parties are reasonably happy.

So why is the anchoring effect so instrumental in decision-making? Well, psychologists think it's linked to our desire to look for confirmation of things we're unsure about. We prefer certainty to uncertainty. For instance, if you see a diamond ring priced at £5,000 you naturally assume it must be worth this much and look for rings of a similar price in other jewellers for confirmation. Unless you're married to me, in which case we're straight home on the bus. Of course, most of us wouldn't be able to tell a £500 ring from one worth £50,000. We need an anchor to give us a guide.

Sometimes the 'anchor' works even when it is manifestly unhelpful, thanks to our fundamental laziness in not wanting to do too much work to make a decision. For example, the first time we realize we massively over paid for that stuffed camel in the souk is when we see it in the really expensive Tax Free airport shop at half the price.

'Anchor!' As my wife said to me when she spotted it.

The truth is, the anchoring effect is everywhere in daily life and we just can't avoid it. In a survey amongst hundreds of real-life credit card users, Neil Stewart of Warwick University showed that among those card holders (36%) who paid more than the minimum payment but less than the total outstanding balance, their choice of how much to pay was correlated with the stated size of the minimum compulsory payment. Participants were given a credit card bill with an outstanding balance of £435 and asked how much they could afford to pay off, given their real-life finances. Crucially, half the participants were shown what the minimum compulsory payment was and half weren't. Among those 45% of participants who said they'd pay only some of the bill, those who saw information on the minimum required payment on the credit card (which was £5.42) said they'd pay off 70% less than those who didn't see information on the minimum payment.

The trick is to be aware of it and try to make it work for you.

Fact is, you don't get what you deserve, you get what you negotiate. That's the first of my 'top tactics' guaranteed to make you a better negotiator. Here are all seven:

1. **The reality**

   You don't get what you deserve, you get what you negotiate. Everyone else wants 'more' too and you will usually get 'more' if you form the cabal and make the other person feel loved, important and part of something. Of course, there are those who want 'WIN–LOSE' but most people who recognize the need for a long-term relationship also have a sense of fairness.

2. **Organ grinder or monkey**

   Before you start to negotiate, make sure the person you're dealing with has the authority to make decisions. Don't let today's multi-layered management systems drive you ape. Often people like to think they are the person with the authority and want you to think that too – it's all part of the need to be important. Don't offend someone by asking what their boss thinks.

Ask them if there's anyone else that needs to be 'involved' in the decision.

3. **Drive the deal**

   Suppose you own a vintage car that someone wants to complete their collection. They need you to sell much more than you need them to buy. Whenever you're in the driving seat, never accept the first offer. Indeed the basic tenets of the negotiation are set by who goes first. If the buyer makes an offer, that's the minimum he's going to pay. If the seller names a price, that's the maximum he's going to get. One man's ceiling is another man's floor in negotiation.

4. **Give an inch to take a mile**

   Nobody expects a concession without offering one in return. So, if you reduce the price to get a sale, make up for it by improving the terms in your favour. Otherwise you're just discounting. If you discount without a reason the buyer is likely to think that you were charging too much in the first place and profiteering, will probably think there is more discount to be had, and won't expect to pay more in the future. Discounting is when you reduce your price with nothing in return. Negotiating is when you use expressions like 'I can't do that but what I can do is ...' or 'If you were able to ... I might be able to ...'.

5. **Walk the walk**

   Give the impression that you're prepared to leave the negotiating table at any time and you'll always end up with the better deal. It's much harder to walk away when you're on your knees begging. The number one rule for holding a high price is to behave like you are worth it. If you can convey the belief that whatever you are offering is worth it and that there is no 'more' to be had they, in turn, will believe that they are getting the best price.

And remember: trying to negotiate after it's all agreed is called begging.

6. **Put time on your side**

Ninety percent of negotiating often occurs in the final ten percent of the time allocated. And time works against the person who doesn't have it. So don't negotiate in a hurry, never reveal your true deadline, always leave your final offer to the last minute and make the last concession a very, very small one. That way the other side feel like there's nothing left. They have achieved their 'more'.

7. **Sell the value, not the cost**

Every salesperson knows that customers attach more value to some things than others, and that 'cost' rarely ever equals 'worth'. So bear this in mind when setting a price. Because people will always pay more for things that they value highly.

In the meantime, can I interest you in a stuffed camel? Great value at just ten quid. Okay, five.

12

The seven things you need to know to improve your communication

Constantly bombarded with messages via a multitude of media, we don't have time to read or listen to an elaborate story that skillfully weaves in a product's features and benefits. Gone are the days of long copy ads in glossy magazines. If you're not on page one on a Google search you're almost certain to be unseen. If your video on YouTube doesn't have appeal, within less than 30 seconds you're toast.

So if you want people to believe what you say in a presentation and ultimately remember what you've said, don't go for flowery introductions or long rambling sentences that just seem to go on endlessly without saying anything very much.

Like that one.

Irony eh?

I spoil you sometimes.

I know that painting a 'vivid picture' seems to contradict the advice to shy away from using elaborate, flowery words. But you can be just as vivid using

concrete facts as with fanciful notions. And this very
fact was proven by a 2010 study by Jochim Hansen
of New York University and the unfortunately named
Michaela Wänke of the University of Basel. They
asked participants to read one of the two statements
set out below and to say whether or not they thought
it was true. Here are the statements:

1. Hamburg is the European record holder con-
   cerning the number of bridges.
2. In Hamburg, one can count the highest number
   of bridges in Europe.

Although both have exactly the same meaning, more
people believed the second sentence than believed
the first. It's not because there's more detail in the
second – there isn't. It's because it doesn't beat
about the bush. It conjures a simple, unambiguous and compelling image: you counting bridges.
Hence, it's more believable. (They did a bit more than
bridges in Hamburg but the findings were always the
same.)

Abstract words are handy for talking conceptually
but they leave a lot of wiggle-room. Whereas concrete words refer to something more precise. For
instance, vanilla ice-cream is specific while dessert
could refer to anything sweet eaten after a main meal.
Verbs as well as nouns can be more or less abstract.
Verbs like 'count' and 'write' are solid, concrete and
unambiguous, while verbs like 'help' and 'insult' are
open to some interpretation. Right at the far end of

the abstract spectrum are verbs like 'love' and 'hate' which leave a lot of room for interpretation.

So, if you want more people to believe you, speak and write solidly and unambiguously. I can't say it any clearer than that.

In summary:

- The more detail and raw fact in a story, the more likely we are to believe it.
- The more vivid a story is, the more we believe it to be true. It's critical that customers believe in your product or service. So everything you say about it, either in person or in print, needs to ring true. And that means using language that is unambiguous. Copywriters are skilled at presenting a product's features and benefits in a way that is clear and concise. They know that this makes any claims more believable.

And it's not only the days of long copy ads in glossy magazines that are gone.

Schooling has changed too. The 'learning to learn' concept has been introduced. It teaches children how to learn the things that they should be learning if they weren't studying how to learn. Then there's all the ground-breaking initiatives that are enthusiastically introduced and quietly withdrawn a few years later. Like not bothering to correct spelling or grammar because it inhibits creative thinking and discourages communication. Well, as you can see, it's never stopped me. Not ever. Never.

So why do I mention this? Well if, like me, you're ever called upon to give a presentation, you might be tempted to cede to the current fad known as 'Allowing for people's different learning styles'. Despite what they may tell you on a presentation skills course, it's poppycock. And I don't care if that's one word or two. Forget about 'building learning systems around the preferred learning style of the audience'. It's nonsense. Just be grateful if they're still awake and facing your way by the end. Maybe even taking notes.

The first clue that 'learning styles' might be just another in a long list of psychobabble is that there are lots of people making money out of it. Consultants will promise to 'measure the preferred learning styles' of your people and then 'help you design training modules to match'.

Complete *couilles*, if you'll pardon my French.

They usually cite the VARK model designed by the Kiwi, Neil Fleming, who thinks that learning styles can be split into four basic types; Visual, Aural, Reading and Writing, and Kinaesthetic. That last one means doing stuff like using a keyboard to learn to play the piano.

I kid you not.

And all these years I've been trying to get a tune out of the ironing board.

Anyway, Frank Coffield of the University of London did a thorough analysis of all the 'learning style models' and found that there are 70 different ways to get information into the brain.

Seventy!

And the real problem is that the only way to establish someone's 'preferred learning style' is to ask them. And that's a bit like asking the fashion-challenged to look in the mirror and then answer the question 'Why?'

They won't know. It's just what happens every day when they get dressed.

So here's the bottom line. The thing that ought to influence the way you present is not the audience but the subject. For instance, the best way to communicate the vastness of Australia is to do it visually with an image of Australia superimposed on a map of Europe. Don't talk numbers of square miles – show them a map. If the subject is dance or how to use an iPod then we need to teach that kinaesthetically. Touch it, feel it, work it out.

People may learn in different ways, but it's what you teach them that really matters.

And you have to repeat things if you want to make sure the message is hammered home.

The idea that something can be drummed into a person by repetition starts when we first attend school.

Learning how to count, the letters of the alphabet, the 12 times table, are all taught by going over the same thing time and time again.

Like me, you've probably never worked out if eleven 11s really are a 121 – we just assume it to be true. But how important is repetition in the art of persuasion? Surely, you can't change the mind of a sceptic simply by repeating something over and over?

Well, yes you can. No, really, you can. I won't tell you again. That's why advertisers spend millions airing a TV campaign that guarantees a certain number of 'opportunities to see'. It's why politicians use the same buzz words over and over. In one of his first speeches as Prime Minister, David Cameron used the term 'values' 12 times in 5 minutes. Sloppy speech writing? No, he just wanted to communicate the idea that his party was all about values. Even the media repeat stories time and again until we believe them. That's how Chris Jefferies, the landlord of the murdered Bristol woman Jo Yeates, became the prime suspect for the crime in 2010. The popular press told us he was guilty and everyone agreed. And then it wasn't so obvious. And everyone agreed again.

Psychological research proves that repetition is one of the easiest methods of persuasion. Apparently, people only need to hear something twice to believe it to be more valid than something they hear only once. We're that easily convinced. According to a study by Ian Begg of the McMaster University in Ontario, people are even more likely to believe a statement by a known liar if it concurs with what someone else has said.

The truth is, repetition makes us believe something is true even when it isn't. As we discussed in a previous chapter, it's widely believed that the team playing away first in a two-legged football match has an advantage. But the stats don't back this up. Yet because pundits continually tell us it's so, we believe it. This is what psychologists call the 'illusion of truth effect' and it arises because of the way our mind works. If we hear something repeatedly it becomes familiar. And we like the familiar. And because familiar things require less effort to process, we assume them to be true.

If your argument is strong don't be afraid to repeat it often and with gusto. And if you can get the audience to retrieve the information from memory at a later date, all the better. Because research shows that this is just as powerful a persuasive tool as repetition.

If you have a presentation to make then repeat your key point three times. And get the audience to retrieve the information you have given them. Because when an idea is retrieved from memory, this has just as powerful a persuasive effect on us as if it had been repeated twice.

The quote 'I hear and I forget. I see and I remember. I do and I understand' is often attributed to the Chinese philosopher, Confucius. At school, I remember teachers using the phrase 'in one ear and out the other' to describe a pupil's lack of learning power. But if Confucius was right, it was probably more to do with a lack of *aides-memoire* rather than a deficiency in 'the little grey cells.'

To test the theory that we absorb information more easily when we see it or have to do something, two researchers from the University of Iowa conducted an experiment. James Bigelow and Amy Poremba were convinced that simply listening to information, without any other kind of stimulus, was the least efficient way to take something in. Of course, nobody listened to their theory so they had to do something to prove it.

In their study, they asked people to listen to a variety of sounds, view a series of images, and touch a range of different objects. For example, a person might be asked to watch sport on TV, then listen to some dogs barking outside, and finally touch a coffee cup without actually looking at it.

Call that an experiment? I had three sons who did that every Saturday morning.

Anyway, each participant was then asked to recall what they had seen, heard and done, an hour later, a day later and a week later. Apart from one guy who couldn't remember taking part at all the results proved that people were more likely to recall the things they had seen or done far more readily than those they had simply heard. In fact, as time went by, they remembered less and less of what they had heard but could still recall with the same level of accuracy a lot of the things they had seen or done.

Not only does the brain use separate pathways to process information, it also processes auditory information differently than visual and tactile data. To improve memory you have to increase mental repetition. Like children learning their times table by saying it out loud over and over again.

It seems that all that hard work creating visual material such as videos or PowerPoints really does pay off – PROVIDING IT'S JUST ENOUGH – when it comes to helping people remember information. So the next time you need to make an important presentation, by all means talk in depth about the subject, but don't forget to back it up with a few, simple visual aids and support it with summarized text. (I'm talking about less than seven words on a slide here.)

And if you're a really tactile person, you might even invite people to come up and touch you.

However, a word of warning from the wise one. Confucius, he also say 'Do not do to others what you do not want done to yourself.' So best to proceed with caution on that last suggestion.

And finally if, like me, your further education took place in the pre-digital age, then you may recall with fondness that quaint old custom of taking notes with the good old-fashioned pen and paper. Back then a note pad really was a note pad. Today it's more likely to be the name of the software that works like a note pad on your iPad.

But a recent study suggests that it might actually be a backward move in terms of helping us to understand and recall the information recorded.

Two researchers from Princeton University decided to test the theory. Pam Mueller and Daniel Oppenheimer got students to watch a filmed lecture and then asked them questions about it. Half of the students made notes with pen and paper and the other half on a laptop. Two types of questions were asked: the first were 'factual recall' questions, such as 'Approximately how many years ago did the Indus civilisation exist?' The second type were known as 'conceptual application' and included questions like 'How do Japan and Sweden differ in their approach to equality within their societies?'

The results showed there was little difference in factual recall between the two sets of note takers.

However, it was a very different story when it came to the student's conceptual understanding. In fact, you could say the gap was the size of a yawning chasm perhaps created by an atomic explosion in a desert wasteland. But that would be insensitive. Anyway, suffice to say, it was a very big gap and proved that the paper-and-pen note takers had retained a significantly larger proportion of conceptual information than their keyboard-thumping counterparts.

Why so? Well, the researchers concluded it was due to the mental processes involved in each technique. The laptop users tended to just transcribe what they heard verbatim, whereas the pen-and-paper brigade 'processed' more of the information. In other words, they selected the important bits and re-wrote them in a shortened format. According to the experts, this enabled them to study the content more efficiently.

So it seems that the best advice to all you modern-day electronic note takers, is to distil the information into a shortened format just as you would if you were writing in long hand. This will embed it in your memory and better aid recall. I could go on, but my trusty quill has just run out of pig's blood. Typical.

So the seven things to remember in order to improve how you communicate when presenting are:

1. Don't beat about the bush at the beginning.
2. The more detail and raw fact in a story, the more likely we are to believe it.

3. Tell a story and make it vivid.
4. It's not the audience that dictates how you present, it's the subject.
5. Know what your main point is.
6. Repeat your main point.
7. And if you want to remember more yourself, use pen and paper.

13

The truth about money and motivation

P laying games teaches us many things about human nature and how we're all different. Some people are very competitive, others less so. Some are good losers, others very bad. You only have to observe the post-match interviews with certain football managers to know how they might react if, during a game of Monopoly, they had the misfortune to land on your Mayfair property complete with two hotels. José Mourinho would doubtless sulk and claim it's a stitch up. Happy Harry Redknapp, however, would probably smile and pay up – albeit using money from his dog's Swiss Bank account. Whilst Arsène Wenger would simply shrug his shoulders and claim not to have seen anything.

The truth is they all love playing mind games and they all have their own individual strategies. Which brings me to the Ultimatum Game. Loved in equal measure by both psychologists and economists alike, it says much about human behaviour and our approach to money. The game is played between two people who have to decide how to split an amount of money. One is randomly chosen to make an offer, and if this is accepted by the other, they each get their agreed share.

However, if the offer is rejected, neither of them gets a penny. It's as simple as that.

So, if you were playing the Ultimatum Game and £1,000 was at stake, how much would you offer the other person? And if you were the other person, how much would you have to be offered to accept? Well, in my studies of doing this in seminars, most people who agreed an offer (pretty much everyone), split the cash after the person doing the offering had offered between 50% and 20% of the £1,000. That's to say, whilst most people offer around 50%, quite often the person doing the offering suggests the other person receiving gets only 40% or even 20% of the amount. But the other person is pretty much always happy to accept. Well, maybe not happy, but they accept all the same. Of course, they could have rejected the offer but then neither would have got a share of the free money. And £200 is better than nothing.

But here's the thing that excites psychologists. When offered 20% or less, more and more people reject it even though this means they get nothing. This proves how humans are economically irrational – particularly when their blood is boiling. It might also explain why gamblers find it hard to cut their losses. It makes no sense to continue but they do so anyway. In the case of the Ultimatum Game, it seems that our sense of injustice kicks in with the offer of such a derisory sum. So we elect to punish the other person's greed by rejecting it, even though neither then gets a share. Incidentally, when I ask the 'offerers' why they offered £500 when they were presumably confident that they could keep more of the £1,000, they talk about 'fairness'. They are driven by the need to avoid making the other person (who in theory they don't know and will never meet) feel unimportant. They feel they are in this game together and are part of a team for the moment.

Economists point out that players of the Ultimatum Game forget it's a one-shot deal. Being 'fair' doesn't matter since the other person can only accept or reject the offer. All you have to do is work out the minimum they're likely to accept. Hence why a stolen TV will be sold for a tenner in a pub car park. It's got nothing to do with value or fairness. If the thief needs the money badly enough, he'll take it.

The good news is that the game demonstrates that most people act fairly, or at least want others to see them acting fairly. And this is a highly rational custom in a society where we have to work together and don't like cheats to prosper. Of course, what the Ultimatum Game ultimately demonstrates is how many psychological complexities can be drawn from a very simple game. And the key point is this – it's not just about the money.

You might think that the more money an employee earns, the happier and more motivated they will be. Apparently, this is nonsense. According to Tim Judge of the University of Florida, higher pay rarely leads to better results. His study of 15,000 individuals suggests that the link between money, motivation and performance is much more complex. In fact, he concluded that even if companies let people set their own salary level, they still wouldn't enjoy the job more. I for one would be worried sick about whether I could still afford myself.

Tim and his team of enthusiastic yet grossly underpaid helpers found that the association between salary and job satisfaction is very weak. What's more, it's a worldwide phenomenon that not only affects the low paid but high earners too. A Gallup survey into employee engagement interviewed 1.4 million people at every pay level, across every industry, in no less than 34 countries. And they too concluded that job satisfaction has little to do with money. They could have stopped after two countries but they enjoyed the work so much.

So does money motivate? Well, naturally, everyone wants to earn enough to pay the mortgage, look after the family, and have enough left over for life's essential luxuries. Like two weeks on a yacht in the Bahamas, a winter break Down Under, plus a lady that comes in to provide a much needed neck massage every Tuesday. Really? That's just me? Are you sure? Blimey.

Anyway, according to the experts, the more people focus on their salary, the less attention they give to the things that actually make them perform better: satisfying their intellectual curiosity, learning new skills, and surprise, surprise, having fun at work. In some instances, money actually demotivates us.

Arnold Schwarzenegger once said: 'Money doesn't make you happy. I now have $50 million but I was just as happy when I had $48 million.' Thanks for that, Arnie.

The theory goes that if salary and bonus is too much of an incentive, people focus on the money rather than on thinking 'outside the box'. And once they stop doing that they become far less effective. The best way to motivate people is to pay them a fair wage and make them feel valued within the company. That way they concentrate on the work, rather than the money. Salesperson of the Week, Employee of the Month, Rear of the Year, are all valuable rewards that motivate yet cost nothing. I particularly cherished that last one which still has pride of place on my mantelpiece.

But don't start celebrating just yet. Because even when you do all that you're not quite home and hosed. There's still one really important factor in making people feel engaged, happy and motivated.

You.

Or, to be more precise, your management team. Competent leaders who provide good direction and focus are the number one influencers when it comes to motivating a workforce to perform at the highest level. And, of course, bad leadership is the biggest single cause of disengagement and disenchantment amongst workers.

But what about financial bonuses to motivate people at work? Well, in recent times, a lot of criticism has been aimed at top executives and their exorbitant salaries. Much of this has been directed towards the banking sector where bonus payments seem to bear no relation to actual performance. In fact, the worse they do, the more they seem to get paid. Not surprisingly, the phrase 'reward for failure' has been a popular tabloid headline.

So why do companies continue to pay huge bonuses to people who consistently underperform? And why isn't all that financial inducement motivating them to do better? Surely offering more money is the best incentive there is? Well, apparently not. And in case you needed more proof than Britain's ailing banks and fat cat bosses, researcher Dan Ariely and his colleagues at Duke University decided to conduct a study.

They asked three groups of economic graduate students from Narayanan University to go to local villages near Madurai in Southern India and ask subjects to perform a series of tasks. The tasks required the participants to use skills such as attention, memory, concentration and creativity. For example, one task was to play a memory game whilst throwing tennis balls at a target. Another involved assembling a puzzle whilst throwing a wellington boot at the life size image of a banker. That was a particularly popular one.

Since the aim was to prove that performance doesn't improve when more money is offered, each of the three groups was incentivized at different levels. One group was offered one day's pay to do well, the second was offered two weeks' pay to do well and the third group a whopping five months' pay to do well.

In other words they rewarded the same level of success with different levels of financial payments.

You may have already guessed the outcome of the experiment. Groups one and two performed at exactly the same level as each other, despite the second being incentivized at ten times the rate of pay. And group three, who could have trousered five months' pay, performed worst of all.

So why is this? According to psychologists, 'super-sized' incentives can be cognitively distracting. The theory goes that there's so much at stake, it impairs performance rather than improves it. In high-pressure situations some people tend to either panic or choke. Panic is when you don't think enough about something and plunge right in – like when you panic buy. Choking is about thinking too much and suffering a loss of instinct. According to Ariely this is what happened to the students who were offered the biggest cash incentive. They thought too much about the task in hand, as well as how bad they were going to feel if they failed to take advantage of this chance in a lifetime.

So, if a cash incentive is no guarantee of improved performance, what is? Well, an experiment by Dean

Karlan involving people determined to stop smoking suggests that 'commitment contracts' are a better bet. According to Karlan, there are two kinds of motivation: intrinsic and extrinsic. The first kind comes from within a person, such as their passion for the task, the pleasure they derive from it and their sense of moral value. Whereas extrinsic motivation is provided externally and usually involves earning money or some other kind of valuable reward.

Researchers discovered that monetary compensation practically kills any kind of creativity. On the other hand, it does motivate people to perform mechanical tasks at a faster rate. Hence the reason why workers in factories and farms often get paid piecemeal. As a student, I once spent a summer picking asparagus. The pay was lousy but the tips were great.

To back this up, an analysis of 51 studies by the London School of Economics found overwhelming evidence that financial incentives may actually reduce an employee's natural inclination to complete a task as well as derive pleasure from it. Perhaps more importantly, it also suggests that any ethical reasons are greatly diminished, such as complying with workplace social norms and fairness. Which would explain why a lot of fat cats don't seem to give a bugger.

So, does money incentivize people? The answer appears to be 'yes' if it's not too much for the individual, but 'no' if it's so large that you can't think about anything other than protecting it. As Henry Kissinger once said: 'Power corrupts. Absolute power corrupts absolutely.'

Not only does paying big bonuses have no direct correlation to better performance, cash often doesn't work as well as gifts as an EXTRA incentive for employees for three reasons.

1. **Cash is considered 'just' income.**
   Fifty quid will go in all directions, and none of it seems worth much. But a piece of merchandise, bought in bulk at £50 a piece, will have a much higher value in perception. To win a meal for two at a nice restaurant or win a free half day's holiday is a great motivator for some people.
2. **Cash has no 'trophy value' or lasting effect.**
   When was the last time somebody showed you their pay cheque? If somebody wins an award they'll tell everyone they know and say how proud they are. Awards make people feel important and also give them that sense of belonging. Award winners often form their own 'cabal' and feel they are part of success.
3. **Cash programmes usually lack goals.**
   'Do your best' is not a goal. Without a specific target there's a risk people will just try a little harder but then tire of doing exactly that.

Money matters. And the vast majority of people want more. But it's the other six drivers that *really* make us tick.

Conclusion: Our seven psychological 'drivers' and the pursuit of happiness

In the introduction we looked at the seven psychological drivers – the things that motivate us all to do what we want to do, and how we do it.

This book has been about how to influence people and how we are influenced. We have looked at why and how people do what they do and, if we are able to get people to do what we want them to do and feel 'motivated' ourselves, then we are in the pursuit of happiness. Good relationships make people happy. And poor relationships usually make both people unhappy. An ongoing corrosive relationship at work can affect even the most thick-skinned of people. So improving your relationships is not just about influencing people but also about becoming happier yourself.

In 2013 the findings of the English Longitudinal Study of Ageing were published. It was a study of over

12,000 people's lives over a period of years. Professor Michael Marmot was principal investigator and the study was a collaboration between University College London, the University of Cambridge and the UK Government. In essence it told us that happy people live longer and, indeed, those recorded as having greater enjoyment of life were likely to die approximately ten years later than other participants. So not only the *quality* of your life but the actual *length* of your life depends on your happiness. You are more likely to live a better, happier, more fruitful life and live longer by understanding the seven psychological drivers and what we each need to do to *be* happy. So let's look at the seven psychological drivers again and what we can do to maximize our happiness.

Drivers 1, 2 and 3: The need to be loved, to be important and to belong

To love and be loved is an essential part of happiness and to feel that you are making a contribution – and therefore being important to others – is key. That means that we all need to cultivate a passion. It could be thoroughly enjoying work or it could be something that you enjoy doing and absorbs you. If you are absorbed in something that has a purpose and meaning, happiness is a by-product of that. You have to follow your arrow wherever it points, do whatever floats your boat and find meanings in the things that you do. Whatever it is, you need to be part of a team so that you enjoy the belonging, make an unselfish contribution so that you get your feeling of importance (without simply wanting to *be* important) and you become loved by others because you are making a contribution.

You need to have a sense that you're unique and that you matter, but are at the same time connected to a bigger organism. Family is usually the base of this but it can be any community, club, society, academic centre or sports club.

Research tells us that people are best protected against certain physical diseases, such as cancer and heart disease, by being part of a community of some kind and being socially involved. The more connected you are and the more you're involved with people, the more likely you are to be happy and live longer.

In Cleveland, researchers at Case Western Reserve University asked men with a history of angina and high blood pressure 'Does your wife show her love?' Those who answered 'no' suffered almost twice as many angina episodes in the next five years as those who replied 'yes'.

Women who view their marriages as strained and have regular hostile interactions with their partners are more likely to have significantly elevated blood pressure and high levels of stress hormones compared to women in happy marriages. Another study found women who had had a heart attack saw a threefold higher risk of having another one if there was discord in their marriage.

Psychologist Janice Kiecholt-Glasier of Ohio State University had newly-weds fight, then took blood samples over the next few hours. She found that the more belligerent and contentious the partners were, the higher the level of stress hormones and the more depressed the immune system. The effect persisted for up to 24 hours.

In another study, Kiechold-Glasier used a vacuum pump to produce small blisters on the hands of women volunteers and then had them fight with their husbands. The nastier the fight, the longer it took for the women's skin to heal.

The quality of our relationships is a big factor in how mentally and emotionally healthy we are. We have an epidemic of anxiety and depression in our most affluent societies despite us becoming more affluent. Fact is, criticism from loved ones increases self-doubt, increases the sense of helplessness and triggers depression.

Simply holding the hand of a loving partner can affect us profoundly. That action can literally calm jittery neurons in the brain. Psychologist Jim Coan of the University of Virginia told women patients having a MRI brain scan that when a little red light on the machine came on, they might receive a small electric shock on their feet, or they might not. Not surprisingly, this information lit up the stress centres in patients' brains. But when partners held their hands, patients registered less stress, and when they were shocked, they experienced less pain.

This is the power of love, to quote Jennifer Rush. We NEED to be loved, we NEED to feel like we are important in some way and we NEED to belong

Drivers 4 and 5: The need to believe and the need for a balance of certainty and uncertainty

The only thing that's constant is change and change is important in our lives. People who are frightened of change are rarely happy, and certainly people who believe that there shouldn't be change – but find it happening all around them – become fearful. The expression 'if you always do what you've always done, you'll always get what you've always got' is just plain wrong. If you just continue to do what you've always done you'll get *less* because everything around you is changing.

Happy people typically don't sit around. They get involved and accept the need to change. They embrace new things but not *all* things. We all need variety in our life, we all need some flexibility in our approach to life and we need to expect the unexpected and the fact that it will challenge us.

Of course we need to believe certain things will be constant in our lives. We want to be confident of our job, our home, our standing in society. But although we continue to believe that certain things will be constants in our lives, we also look for a balance of certainty and uncertainty which is right for us. If you personally enjoy going on holiday to the same place every year, then keep going to that place. If you can only get your thrills from extreme sports, go and do that; but believe in something and always have a balance of certainty and uncertainty in your life.

Driver 6: The need for 'a place'

A survey by the UK Government published in 2014 concluded that the happiest workers were members of the clergy. Vicars, priests, ministers, rabbis and so on – men and women of the cloth of all denominations – were happiest and got the most satisfaction from their jobs.

What emerged from the research was that whilst there was a link between earnings and life satisfaction, some quite well-paid jobs were populated by those with low levels of wellbeing and vice versa. It echoed a study done by the University of Chicago in 2007 that concluded that not only were the clergy the happiest people, but the most satisfying jobs generally were from professions involving caring for, teaching and protecting other people. The survey was the most comprehensive of its kind to explore satisfaction and happiness amongst American workers and it's worthwhile as we come towards the end of the book to examine why it is that the clergy are so happy.

Well, they feel loved, they feel important and they have a great sense of belonging to their 'congregation'. They have a very strong belief, they have a balance of certainty and uncertainty in their life and, importantly, they have a place. A place of worship they call their own where they become truly absorbed with a true purpose and meaning to their life.

And they believe that there's more after this life …

Driver 7: The need for growth and improvement

Happy people are content and the contentment comes from being happy. But you need to accept it's a natural desire to want 'more'. That could be to learn and develop intellectually, to grow a career or even grow vegetables, you may want more money, a better golf handicap, to be slimmer, to have more friends or just to be happier. In an important study by Daniel Gilbert of Harvard, he found that the vast majority of people think that they will be happier in the future than they are right now.

He may well be right, but if you are waiting for happiness to arrive in the future you're missing the glorious now. You need to milk the sacred now but have a plan to improve in the area that's important to you so that you have hope and you can achieve more. This makes you happier right now.

And the people at the bottom of the scale in both of these surveys were people who didn't feel they were appreciated in their job, didn't feel important and had no plan for the future to give them more. So the pursuit of happiness for you is to look at what drives you. You have to accept the things you cannot change and change the things you can. You need to work on loving relationships and become important without pursuing importance for its own sake. You need a balance of certainty and uncertainty in your life that suits you and you need to have hope. Hope for a better future no matter how good your life is now, because the only thing that's constant is change.

US Researchers have discovered that the more sports teams practise, the better they get. No, really. Apparently, levels of skill, fitness and teamwork all improve greatly resulting in more matches being won. But hold your horses. If you don't have one handy, hold something similar. The research goes on to suggest that the benefits of 'persistent practise' dissipate after about four years. Think Spain in the football World Cup. Winners in 2010, first team knocked out in 2014. Crikey, they might be on to something.

After four years, the theory goes that experience and practise lead to over-confidence, complacency and routine rigidity. But this isn't a new theory. Over 2,000 years ago Aristotle, the Greek philosopher and head coach of all their national sports sides, said something very similar. Only in Greek, obviously.

He declared that both 'excessive and defective exercise destroys the strength'. He went on to say: 'Similarly, drink or food above or below a certain amount destroys the health, whilst that which is proportionate both increases and preserves it.' So basically, he was championing the idea of moderation in everything. Including moderation.

Or, put another way, practise makes perfect but you can also have too much of a good thing.

Now fast forward over 2,000 years and you can see how in business today the relationship between experience and performance sometimes takes the form of an inverted U. Companies often enjoy a period of great success just before a quick slide into decline.

Same people, same product, same market, but different results. Whereas companies and individuals who constantly reinvent themselves often enjoy continued success. Think Branson. Music, banking, trains, planes – quite probably more to come in the future.

In our personal life, it's clear that ongoing happiness and success lie somewhere between the extremes of deficiency and excess. In philosophy it's often known as 'The Golden Mean'. It's difficult to be truly happy if you are constantly in need, particularly if those around you seem to have more than you.

There is quite a considerable body of evidence that shows people actually evaluate 'consumption' on a relative rather than an absolute basis. That is, people evaluate their personal satisfaction and overall happiness by comparing themselves to others they know. So the person who had three yachts and now only has two may be less happy than the person who had none but now has one. And the person who had three will very definitely be unhappy if all his yacht-buying friends are onto their fourth yacht.

A couple of academics, Philip Brickman and Donald Campbell, took this concept to its natural conclusion with their rather charmingly entitled 'hedonic treadmill hypothesis' which proposed that improvements in our circumstances bring only temporary increases in happiness. Basically, over time we adapt our reference points to incorporate the improvements and eventually evaluate our circumstance in relation to the new status quo. So going back to yacht buying again, their theory suggests that a person acquiring his first yacht experiences an unusual amount of happiness only until he becomes used to owning it. After that, he is no happier than he was before he owned it. You may well have had the same experience when you've bought a new car.

In self-presentation, 'honesty' is the mid-point between self-deprecation and arrogant boasting.

Those around you don't want you moaning and putting yourself down all the time, but neither do they want you to be constantly showing off. Even in telling someone about your great holiday or a fabulous wedding you've attended you can be too short or drag on too long. I often say to people, do you want the 60 second version of my holiday or the half hour one? No prizes for guessing their choice.

Similarly, 'friendliness' is the mean between being argumentative and trying too hard to ingratiate oneself.

The inverted U theory is a widespread phenomenon in psychology. In fact, there's plenty of research to indicate that happiness can be boosted by gratitude exercises, such as counting one's blessings and delivering 'thank you' messages. Even having a Positive Mental Attitude is thought to enhance performance and creativity. Visualize the goal, see yourself crossing the finishing line, etc. But try not to go straight to spending the money.

However, all the recent evidence suggests that whereas moderate levels of positive emotions *enhance* creativity, high levels do not. Apparently, intense positivity often leads to a detrimental psychological effect. For example, extremely cheerful people often engage in riskier behaviours and therefore live shorter lives. Which doesn't explain why my wife looked so glum when I surprised her with that bungee jump present last Christmas.

The survey by Tim Judge I mentioned in the chapter on money and motivation concluded that the association between salary and job satisfaction is very weak indeed. He calculated that there is less than 2% overlap between pay and job satisfaction levels. Furthermore, the correlation between pay and pay satisfaction was only marginally higher, indicating that people's satisfaction with their salary is mostly independent of their actual salary.

It's whether people's psychological drivers are met that really gives people satisfaction at work and overall happiness ...

Further comparisons revealed that the relationship of pay to both job and pay satisfaction is pretty much the same everywhere (for example, there are no significant differences between the Britain, the USA, India, Australia and Taiwan).

So in summary, every dog has his day but good things don't last forever. Play to the gallery but always leave them wanting more. You can have your cake and eat it, but remember all that glitters is not gold. And finally, practise makes perfect but familiarity breeds contempt.

And if you still don't know when you've 'done enough' and it's time to stop, here's one final clue. It was probably just before you said to yourself 'I've done enough'.

Enough said.

The top 50 questions for you to master influence and persuasion

1. What is the most important thing to you about ... ?
   Why is that?

2. What is the most frustrating thing for you about ... ?
   Why is that?

3. Why do you ask?

4. I wonder if you could help me?

5. If you were me, what would you do?

6. What makes you say that?
   (What draws you to that conclusion?/Can you give me some background on that?)

7. How do you feel about that?

8. How was yours?

9. What are your expectations exactly?

10. What is the most pressing issue facing you in the business right now?

11. What is the purpose of the meeting exactly?

12. What is the ONE thing I can I do to help you today?

13. Is there any aspect of our service we could improve on?
(Can you tell me *one* thing we could do better?)

14. Is there something you could have done better yesterday?

15. What do you think causes ... ?
(Do you have a perspective on that?)

16. Was there a particular event that made you think differently?
(When was the first time you noticed ... ?
/When was the last time you actually ... ?)

17. Is it for someone special?

18. What have you done so far to address the problem?

19. What would you do differently if ... ?
(What would we do differently if ... ?)

20. How important is that to you?/Why does that matter to you exactly?

21. Who benefits most from ...?

22. How are ... and ... similar?

23. What is likely to happen if … ? / What won't happen if … ?

24. Can I ask you three questions?

25. What are the implications for you if … ? (What else does that affect?)

26. Would it be useful/helpful if … ?

27. What are your aspirations exactly?

28. In an ideal world what would you have?/What would success look like for you? What would make this perfect for you?

29. Have you chatted to anyone else about this?

30. Is anyone else involved in the buying decision?

31. What are the key drivers for the other people involved?

32. Whose opinion matters most about this would you say?

33. What are the benefits you would see as a result of this worth to you … ?

34. If you are looking at two other options for this, could you rank them for me?

35. What are the strengths and weaknesses of … ?

36. Which one do you like the least?

37. Which would be easiest for you?

38. If I were to ... could you ... ?

39. Is there anything else we need to consider? (So if you like x, y and z, is there anything else we need to consider?)

40. On a scale of 1 to 10 (with 10 being high)
    ... how important is it to you?
    ... how likely is it that this will help you?
    ... how likely are you to go ahead?

41. Why is it not less than that? (Why did you not pick a lower number?)

42. What do we have to do to get to 10?

43. Just out of curiosity, what is it that ... ?

44. I agree you should think about it. Often when our clients say that it's because there is a particular issue they need to address. Is that the case with you?

45. Is that your best price?

46. Will that be enough for you?

47. Shall we go ahead?

48. Would you like something with that?

49. What is it that we currently don't provide that, if we did, you would be interested in buying from us?

50. On a scale of 1 to 10, how likely are you to recommend us to a friend?

About the author

Philip Hesketh set up his own advertising agency in the UK and sold it after 16 consecutive years of growth with the agency billing £48m and employing 150 people.

Having spent his entire working life studying and practising influence and persuasion, he is now a full-time professional speaker on 'The Psychology of Persuasion and Influence'. He combines a powerful mix of well-researched stories with a unique brand of humour. He inspires, entertains and gives 'can-use-today' techniques to be more influential both in people's business and personal lives. He is inspirational, motivational and thought provoking.

For more details see: www.heskethtalking.com

Index

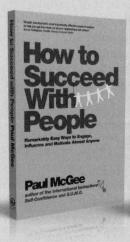

get
more

Your monthly dose of business brilliance - articles, interviews, videos and more

Sign up to our newsletter today!